SAVE MONEY AND SPEND WISELY

DURING AND AFTER CORONAVIRUS

Personal Finance Tips for Managing Money and Budgeting Wisely during the COVID-19 Crisis

—————— **DANA WISE** ——————

© Copyright Dana Wise 2020 - All rights reserved.

The content contained within this book may not be reproduced, duplicated or transmitted without direct written permission from the author or the publisher except for the use of brief quotations in a book review.
Under no circumstances will any blame or legal responsibility be held against the publisher, or author, for any damages, reparation, or monetary loss due to the information contained within this book. Either directly or indirectly. You are responsible for your own choices, actions, and results.

Legal Notice:
This book is copyright protected. This book is only for personal use. You cannot amend, distribute, sell, use, quote or paraphrase any part, or the content within this book, without the consent of the author or publisher except for the use of brief quotations in a book review.

Disclaimer notice:
Please note the information contained within this book is for educational and entertainment purposes only. All effort has been executed to present accurate, up to date, and reliable, complete information. No warranties of any kind are declared or implied. Readers acknowledge that the author is not engaging in the rendering of legal, financial, medical or professional advice. The content within this book has been derived from various sources. Please consult a licensed professional before attempting any techniques outlined in this book.
By reading this book, the reader agrees that under no circumstances is the author responsible for any losses, direct or indirect, which are incurred as a result of the use of the information contained within this book, including, but not limited to,—errors, omissions, or inaccuracies.

SAVE MONEY AND SPEND WISELY

DURING AND AFTER CORONAVIRUS

Personal Finance Tips for Managing Money and Budgeting Wisely during the COVID-19 Crisis

DANA WISE

Table of Contents

7   Introduction

13 **Chapter One:** *Know Thyself: Spending and Goals*

27 **Chapter Two:** *Focus on Food*

41 **Chapter Three:** *Pandemic-Proof Your Home Costs*

57 **Chapter Four:** *Wired for Smart Budgeting*

67 **Chapter Five:** *Entertainment That's Fun and Frugal*

85 **Chapter Six:** *Revisit Your Vehicles*

99 **Chapter Seven:** *Dress to Impress (Your Wallet)*

111 **Chapter Eight:** *Travel Tight*

119 **Chapter Nine:** *Create Your Future Today*

127 **Chapter Ten:** *Continue Saving*

135 Final Words

139 Leave a Review

140 My Other Book You Will Love

141 Resources

SAVE MONEY AND SPEND WISELY DURING AND AFTER CORONAVIRUS

Your one-page form

 **I will save on** *My car consumption*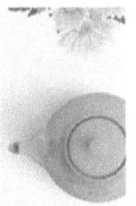

The form will lead you step-by-step

	DONE
Actions and SMART goals that you will achieve	✓
Maximize your immediate saving	✓
Save many thousands every year	✓
BONUS: non-financial benefits for your dream life	✓

rsagile.activehosted.com/f/3

DANA WISE

INTRODUCTION

DO you find the current economic upheaval scary? Not sure what to do about it? Well, you're not alone! It's not clear what the ultimate impact will be, but despite the uncertainty, there are still many things that you can do personally to manage your money wisely during this time.

As of now (March 2020), we don't know how long the current restrictions will last, and like plenty of others, you may not have any income coming in. Unfortunately, what we do know is that bills will continue despite that lack of income! There may be some relief coming in from different institutions, but for the most part, bills must be paid on the savings we already have.

That doesn't mean all is lost, however. You can decide to spend wisely now and consider your purchases carefully before you buy them. There are some immediate solutions you can put into place, along with medium and long-term steps you can take to shore up your financial situation.

Human brains prefer certainty, which is partly why the current atmosphere feels so frightening with all the unknowns in the air. Once you develop a plan for your finances, however, you'll find that life no longer seems so uncertain. Managing your money means that you are taking control of your funds, and our brains like that feeling of control! I like it as well as you!

Once you've started saving money using the practical tips provided within this book, you will find saving money will be much easier for you. Even if you found it difficult before, and especially if you had never really paid attention to your personal finances, you will discover why it's important for developing a mastery of your money.

Your money is a tool—nothing more. It doesn't define who you are as a person, and it shouldn't run your life. Learning how to use this tool properly will not only help you get through this economic upheaval relatively unscathed. In doing so, you will also greatly empower yourself.

Many people avoid thinking about their money or try to manage it proactively because they don't like numbers or math. Again, good news! The biggest factor to successful money management is actually your mindset, and you will learn how to think about your finances correctly and avoid bad decisions. That is really the key to personal finance.

In this book, I will be showing you how to achieve that successful money mindset and discussing the importance of goals. It can sometimes be challenging to forego your current spending habits, but it will be much easier once you have something tangible to save for. In some ways, the current coronavirus epidemic may actually help you spend less money. With bars, restaurants, and movie theaters shut down for an unknown period of time, you will have fewer places to spend money unthinkingly.

One essential tip for managing your money wisely is to know exactly how you're spending money. Many people, after monthly payments for rent, utilities, and other fixed costs, don't really know how they should spend the rest of their income. You will learn how to track your spending and figure out where all that money went. We will also be discussing the importance of setting aside an emergency fund, even if you can't manage to save an entire three months' worth of expenses at the moment.

Recognizing what you value will also be incredibly helpful because such will allow you to focus your spending on that and cut back on other expenses. When you don't spend on things you don't really care about, you won't feel as deprived, thus actually allowing you to stick to your spending plan.

Another critical factor in personal finance is recognizing that done is better than perfect. You can't save the maximum for your retirement contribution? That's OK, you can save a little, which is better than none. Can't cut out all your sports spending? That's OK, you can cut back on the things that you don't necessarily need or want right now.

With the tips in this book, you will learn how to manage your spending once this crisis has passed. And it will, as they always do. You'll come out of the pandemic with solid knowledge about personal finance that you will be able to use to your advantage for the rest of your life. You will understand the difference between wants and needs and learn how to budget for both.

Did you know that understanding a topic gives you power over it? Right now, you may be feeling a bit powerless and thinking that you can do hardly anything in terms of your money. Get ready to change that because reading this book will help you learn how to take action.

In addition to exploring your own goals, we will be going over some practical tips for managing your funds. The chapters about spending are divided into quick actions you can take right now, medium-term suggestions that you can use in the next few months, and long-term advice that may take you a bit more time and effort to add into your daily routines. Toward the end is when we will be discussing how you can take all this knowledge into the future and stay motivated, even when you don't have a financial crisis to spur you on.

I will show you the positive future consequences of the decisions you make today, and you will see the many compounding benefits to receive just from choosing one right decision. The benefits of good decision-making go well beyond saving money—they will also improve other areas of your life, including your mental and physical health and well-being.

It is easy for anyone to implement the tips and ideas from this book into their life, and you don't need to be a finance or math whiz to do them. You probably don't even need a calculator! You just need to know what's important to you. It's not about what other people are spending or even how they are dealing with their money during the crisis; it's about you and your family being smart about it.

Mindless spending happens quite often in a consumerist society, which is what we are living in right now. By the end of this book, you will cease to be another mindless consumer; instead, you will be a savvy spender, and you will be able to maximize your budget for your specific situation.

Right now, you may be wondering—what qualifies me to give you all this advice? How credible am I?

I have been in the financial industry for years and have helped people just like you to take control of their money. I was in finance when we didn't have easy apps to help us balance out the portfolio, track spending, or even round up our spending to invest the difference. Now, it's incredibly easy for people to track their spending without having to write down every expense in a notebook or spreadsheet!

I have spent a lot of time coaching people through their spending plans. Including how to identify the low-hanging fruit on their spending that they can cut back easily without feeling deprived. And, figuring out what is important to them so they can spend appropriately. Many think that people with lots of money know what to do with it, and I can tell you for a fact that that is not true! I have assisted people who have a lot of money, along with those who don't have a lot of money.

Most people I have worked with really didn't know how to handle their finances, no matter their bank balance or how educated they were in finance. It's not a topic taught often in most schools, nor will you really find college courses about it either. However, as a former financial planner, I think everyone should understand the basics of finance!

You may not know this, and most people won't tell you because they don't want you thinking critically about your money, but mindless purchasing costs much more than you would think. Suppose you earned $10; $2 went to taxes, and maybe you saved

$1 for retirement. However, you spent the rest of it. Do you know where that $7 went?

Don't worry—I have ideas for you to save several dollars from each $10 earned without feeling deprived. The quicker you can take control, the better. Doing so will not just help with your finances, but your mental health as well.

Lately, I've seen a lot of people panicking about their money during this time of upheaval. No judgment because it's perfectly understandable! The pandemic response kicked off a recession, which has historically made even the most shrewd investors nervous about their money. I've been through recessions, including the Great Recession of 2008-2009, and helped guide people through it. Our country has been through pandemics before, and it undoubtedly will again.

But you must act now! The longer you wait to learn about and implement these tips, the harder it will be to take action. If you're overspending now on things that don't matter to you, you are literally draining your money faster than you need to. The sooner you can halt the mindless spending and reduce what you spend on "wants," the stronger your finances will be.

The actions I recommend will benefit you both in the short term and long term while making your brain happy. By reading this book, you will learn new actions that you can take right away, so don't hesitate when you have the chance now to triumph over current circumstances.

Today is a great day to create your future, so let's get started!

Chapter ONE

KNOW THYSELF: SPENDING AND GOALS

THIS chapter will focus on creating the right framework for implementing the steps found in the following chapters. Because we will be going over some relevant information for the next sections in this book, it would be a terrible idea to skip this all-important first chapter! If you don't learn why you should cut back on certain items and don't figure out an overall goal to look toward, you will have a lot of difficulty in sticking to your plan.

Have you ever tried to master your money before but ended up splurging, thus depleting your savings? It's pretty common, and it means that you probably didn't know what you really wanted to spend money on, or specifically why you wanted to reduce your spending; you didn't have a concrete goal to work toward.

Not running out of money during the coronavirus crisis may seem like a pretty good reason to avoid spending money, and it absolutely is! There are closures occurring across entertainment, among other businesses. However, if that's your only reason to stop splurging, such a thought process won't help your future behavior once the current crisis is over. You will need another reason that's not influenced by short-term events.

Mindset

We mentioned in the introduction that our brains prefer certainty and action, which are two principal cognitive biases that all humans evolved to have, among plenty of others. Most other biases, however, were adaptations that helped us when we were early humans living on the savannah and needed to worry about where our next meal would be coming from, and whether we ourselves were to become a tiger's next meal!

Those older biases don't necessarily work now in the modern world, however. We may still have our wild savannah-adapted brains in a decidedly non-savannah world, though human beings in developed nations don't really have to worry about where their next meal is coming from. We don't even have to go get it; we can have the next meal delivered to our doorstep with nothing more than a bit of typing, and we are not being stalked by tigers.

However—and especially during a recession and this Coronavirus crisis—we do worry about being capitalism's next meal because that is where the money to pay our bills and keep the lights on and a roof over our heads comes from. Thinking that we can't earn any money because our workplace shut down due to the coronavirus or possibly a recession is a scary thought.

Being frightened is located mainly in the part of our brains that we inherited from our reptilian ancestors, and you may have heard it called **reptilian** or **lizard brain** as a result. It is where we have our *fight-or-flight* reaction, and is also known as the **amygdala**.

The rational part of our brain evolved later. It loves resources and information and works slowly, at least compared to the amygdala. This part of the brain is in the **frontal lobe**, and it helps you evaluate the advantages and disadvantages between certain options you may be considering at any time.

When the body's stress response is activated, your heart beats faster and you may start breathing hard. The stress hormone cortisol is released, and the brain essentially takes the rational portion offline. There's no time for weighing the pros and cons of running away from a tiger because, if you did that, you would probably be eaten. The brain wants to survive, so it activates the fight-or-flight reaction when threatened. However, when the amygdala is in charge, the rational section of the brain won't function well enough to put together an appropriate response.

Why does this matter? Well, our brains can't tell the difference between the fear of being eaten by a tiger and the fear of running out of money. Fear is fear, so the brain releases cortisol, starts to prepare the body to run away from the tiger, taking down those rational functions in the process. This process means that, when you're stressed, panicked, or afraid in terms of current events, you literally cannot think straight.

This fear is completely natural. We're facing an uncertain world, so it would make sense that you are feeling fearful, anxious, and as if you lack control. However, when it comes to making good financial decisions and managing your money, you will need your rational brain in a completely functional state. In some circumstances, that will mean that you work around your fears. There are some tricks you can use to bring your rational thought back online once stressed but need to make decisions.

o The serenity statement

"...grant me the serenity to accept the things I cannot change, the courage to change the things I can, and the wisdom to know the difference." —Reinhold Niebuhr

There are a lot of things in the modern world that we simply have no control over, and this obviously includes certain viruses, including the novel coronavirus! What government leaders will say and do in response to a crisis is not something an individual citizen has control over—the only thing we can do is vote out politicians who don't do their jobs properly.

Stock market returns are beyond our control, at least in the short term. We know that, on average, the stock market returns 8-10% over a long period. However, what it will do in the short term is anyone's guess.

We don't know which businesses will close permanently or what life will look like once the current crisis is over. There is also uncertainty about what exactly our "new normal" will look like. That normal could be similar to life before the coronavirus, but we won't really know until then.

Worrying about these things is completely futile because there's nothing we can do about them. Thinking too much about these topics will cause our amygdala to rule us, which means we'll start making terrible decisions.

Cortisol and the related stress response is fine for us in short bursts, like it was with our ancestors. However, when it's released almost constantly, as it is for some people, it causes long-term damage to your body and shortens your life.

Instead, consider what you can change. You have a vote, so use it when election day rolls around. Don't just consider this for the big national elections, but local ones too. You decide how much you want to save and what you want to spend, unless you're at or below the poverty line. You know what your skills are, and you should learn how to leverage them.

Wisdom comes when you figure out what you have control over and what you can change. It should be pretty obvious that no single individual has any control over the stock market with the billions of trades being executed regularly.

You have no control over what anyone else does. To a certain extent, you even lack control over your own thoughts and emotions! Your brain's job is to generate thoughts, and so it does, but not all of these thoughts are helpful, useful, or relevant. You'll also experience certain feelings, which just happen. Let them happen, because you will get in trouble by trying to repress them!

However, what you can command is your response to these thoughts and feelings. You don't have to react to them right away, if at all. The thoughts that don't serve you can be let go, released onto a leaf in a mental stream flowing away from you, or visualized as a cloud that appears and then disappears.

You may be feeling stressed or scared, which is perfectly fine. However, it's not usually fine to take action based on those emotions before you've thought them through.

- Take control where you can

    Remember that human brains like action and being in control! Therefore, don't spend your valuable time worrying about something that you have no personal influence over. Instead, spend it thinking about the actions you can take to make positive changes.

    Make a plan that will outline how you will be spending your money. Find a place where you can cut back your spending and then just do it. When you do pleasurable things, like taking action, your brain will release a little bit of **dopamine**, which is known as the "feel-good" neurotransmitter. Therefore, when you take that action, you'll feel good.

When you see the results of your actions, you will feel like you're back in control, which will then hit you with another dose of dopamine! Tracking your spending, creating financial goals, and shifting money to better places are all situations that give you pleasure and will help you in the long term.

- **Take deep breaths and do math**

    I know, *I know* I said there wouldn't be any math! However, math is a great way to bring your rational functions back after your stress response takes over.

    Deep breathing is another way to slow down your stress. When you're afraid and getting ready to run away from that tiger, your breathing speeds up because your body needs some quick hits of oxygen for either flight or fight. By slowing your breathing down deliberately, you signal the lack of threat to your amygdala[1] (Goleman, 2005). Your brain, realizing the tiger's gone, will stop its stress response, which allows rational function to take over again. Doing math also brings your "thinking" brain back to the forefront. It doesn't necessarily have to be complicated math; there's no need for calculus unless you really want it.

    Are you making lists of expenses and amounts you want to cut back on, adding up columns of spending, and comparing last month's spending to this month's?

    Human brains are puzzle and problem solvers. If you give your brain a math problem, it will naturally want to solve it. Since the amygdala is quite hopeless when it comes to numbers, rational function will have to start working again to solve the problem.

Know the Differences Between Needs, Desires, and Goals

How many times have you gone shopping and exclaimed *"I need this!"* about something you didn't really need? Probably many times. Whether the object of desire is shoes, a toy, a stereo system, or a new piece of gaming equipment, it's doubtful that you would really need it. You might want it badly, but wanting something a lot does not necessarily equate to needing it.

Most people in developed countries have similar material needs. We won't delve too much into Maslow's hierarchy of needs and self-actualization; instead, we will keep it focused on the physical[2] (Mcleod, 2020). We need a roof over our heads; for example, renting versus owning is an expression of desire—not need. We need enough food to nourish ourselves, along with clothing.

To live in the modern world, we need other things as well. If you live in an area without good public transportation, you will probably need a car to get around. You need electricity and an Internet connection, which would certainly come as a surprise to your great-great-grandfather! The reality is that the modern world creates certain demands that we must abide by to function. You need a phone, though technically a smartphone specifically isn't necessary.

Nearly everything else is a "want." There are tons of *wants* we could go over—wanting to hang out with friends and eat nachos at a sports bar, wanting to go to professional sports games, wanting to own a pet, wanting a state-of-the-art stereo or video game system, or wanting the latest smartphone are all *wants* that you don't necessarily *need*. You may want to browse storefronts or check online stores; however, you don't need to spend money on what you see.

We live in a consumerist society, and we signal our values with what we buy. Although we do need clothing, we don't necessarily need to purchase designer clothes. Expensive designers are a want, not a need. Vehicles are necessary; however, most people don't really need giant SUVs or gas-guzzling pickup trucks, nor do we need that brand new car. Those are desires and ways to show others what's important to us.

What's necessary for most people is just a boring old two or four-door car that has good gas mileage. This year's smartphone is pretty much exactly the same as last year's. Maybe the company added a pixel on the camera, or some other feature that's more or less irrelevant to how you use it. No matter how many new add-ons they implement, you don't actually need to upgrade; you just want to.

Your needs are probably already covered. What was the last thing you wanted to buy? Would you even have room for it? Did you have enough money on hand to pay for it, or did you plan to add it to your credit card and increase the amount of money you owe exponentially? (We'll discuss compound interest shortly).

Think about what your values are, which is probably not mindless shopping. Nevertheless, maybe you're big into the environment and saving the planet. Very few items that you buy will be good for the environment unless you're buying a new energy-efficient washing machine or other similar products.

Is it important to you to spend time with your friends? Hopefully, it is! We humans are naturally social beings, but you don't have to spend tons of money to do that. If that's why you were spending so much money on happy hour, it's easy enough to stop. Invite your buddies over and tell them to bring their own drinks. It's much cheaper to buy from the store instead of paying the markup when you go out, and you can still have more fun at home than at the bar anyway!

Can't go out due to the coronavirus? Consider trying FaceTime, Skype, Zoom, or whatever other similar services are out there. Through video calling, you can still have a virtual party with your friends. You can then switch to house parties once the pandemic is over and restrictions are lifted. I personally expect that people will get used to these new ways of socializing, which will likely become the new norm.

Is fitness important to you? Great! But do you have to join the fanciest and most expensive gym in town? Not necessarily. Instead, try setting up your own gym. Find a cheaper place you can go to when the restrictions are lifted and watch some how-to work out and set up videos online.

For pretty much anything you value, there will be other ways to enjoy it without having to pay so much money. You may argue it's just $20 a month. Although that may be correct, $20 per month turns into $240 per year, or $4,800 after 20 years (not including interest). If you're in the 22% tax bracket here in the US, you would have had to earn over $6,100 to save that much! How valuable is $240 per year during crisis time? Clearly it does have quite a big value.

Spending is the easiest and most mindless way to express your values. Let's try something different.

What are your goals in life? Everyone should be thinking about retirement because you need to save up your own money to avoid being poverty-stricken in old age. No, you won't be able to work forever—at some point, you will no longer be physically or mentally able to work 40 hours a week. Decline starts earlier than most people think, and financial literacy starts dropping at age 60[3] (Finke et al., 2016).

If retirement is the goal, what else might you want to do? Buy a house, stop working for someone else and run your own business? Travel? Write those ideas down. Knowing why you want to cut back on spending (besides cutting back during the coronavirus crisis) will help you get through the times when the short term beckons with cute shoes or powerful game equipment.

I have written a new book *Work from Home During and After Coronavirus* that is complementary to this one. It describes how to earn money as a freelancer or entrepreneur during this crisis and fix your other problem: lack of income. For starting any business, you will need some initial "seed" money to pay your bills until you're profitable. On the other hand, investing in your own business will bear the highest return because you won't have to share that profit with anyone else.

Consequences of Saving vs. Spending

OK, we might need a little math when figuring out our expenses, but we'll keep it simple. Compound interest is something that you cannot control. You can either learn to use it to your advantage or suffer by having others, like credit card companies, use it against you.

Compound interest is basically money growing on itself. If, for example, you have $1,000 that earns a 10% return annually, at the end of one year, you would have $1,100. Then, in the next year, the 10% grows on top of that $1,100; not the original $1,000, and so forth. It takes a little while for compounding to hit its stride—years, not months. Therefore, leaving your money alone can be pretty powerful. Consider a more reasonable scenario in which your $1,000 is earning an average 6% return, as it would if invested in a portfolio that contained more stocks than bonds.

Get to know the Rule of 72, which tells you how long the money takes to double, given a specific return. In the example above, your $1,000 would turn into $2,000 at the end of twelve years (72/6 = 12). Doesn't sound too impressive? Try $10,000. In twelve years, that amount would become $20,000 without you adding to it or even doing anything. You were merely staying away from it and letting it grow. While you can't control the average return of your portfolio, you can influence it by being proactive, which would mean adding stocks.

If you earned 8% on average with an all-stock portfolio, your money would double in 9 years instead of 12. If you left it for 36 years, it would double four times. At a 6% return, it would double only three times.

You also control the time you leave your money to compound for you. It's a good idea to start early and not panic and sell off your stocks when a recession hits. Right now, bonds generate maybe about 3%, which means it would take 24 years to double. If everything's in cash, you will not be earning anything. There would be no compounding at all, and certainly no doubling.

Now, imagine this power working against you. In that case, you would start with a $1,000 debt, which would probably be on your credit cards (student loans and mortgages don't compound in the same way that credit cards do). You wouldn't pay it off. Typical credit cards compound about 24% annually, and your $1,000, if you don't pay it off right away, would be $2,000 in three years. That is all assuming you don't add to it… which is unlikely.

If you have credit card debt, one of your first goals should be to pay it off as soon as you can. Right now during the crisis, doing so may not be possible. Afterward, however, you can do your best to keep your spending cuts in place and use the savings to pay off credit cards and create an emergency fund.

This **emergency fund** will prevent you from adding back to your credit card debt if something were to happen. You need three to six months' expenses in cash in that fund, depending on your situation and how much risk you're comfortable taking (Elkins, 2019).[4]

How Much Are You Spending?

Right now, you may not even recognize just how much you are spending. If you're living paycheck to paycheck, spending your income (other than contributions you make for your savings,

SAVE MONEY AND SPEND WISELY DURING AND AFTER CORONAVIRUS CHAPTER ONE

including retirement), and using credit cards and not paying them off at the end of the month, it means your spending exceeds your income. In either case, you definitely need to cut back, but where would you do that?

First, you need to know where your money is going. There are many online apps that can help you do the tracking without lifting a finger (LaPonsie, 2019).[5] There is little difference between all of them, so pick one that's free and start using it right away.

Search through your current statements to see where your past few months' spending has gone. Some of your expenses may be on necessities such as rent or mortgage, utilities, and groceries. We will be going over proven tips on reducing costs surrounding those too in a bit. Nevertheless, most people find it easier to attack the discretionary items that they want but don't need: mindless shopping, entertainment, and eating out to name a few examples.

Look through how much you spend on your *wants*. Which of these wants match up with what you value, and which of them were just mindless spending? For example, suppose you value spending time with friends, but your credit card statements reveal that you spend often at the priciest clothes store in town or at the game store. You can cut those expenses out without feeling deprived because time with friends is what's important to you.

You may find that some of these expenses are nothing more than habits, and that staying home during the coronavirus might break you of them without you having to do too much! Maybe you were in the habit of going to the local coffee shop during your afternoon break for a little pick-me-up. Now that you are no longer working in your office, you don't need to hit that coffee shop. You might still need a little something in the afternoon, but you can make your own coffee at home without all the sugar and additives. You can also decide to take some time to stretch and breathe deeply, which can be enough to keep you going.

In other words, the key is to only spend money on the things you value (we'll talk about ways to spend less money on them without feeling deprived in the ensuing chapters). No more mindlessly throwing down the credit card for anything that catches your eye. You'll think about your purchases before you make them. Best of all, you'll be enjoying yourself without feeling too deprived, as it is important to feel good, even more so in difficult times. Such will help you continue your new, better habits once the coronavirus is under control.

Chapter Summary

- Mindset and taking control of things that you can influence are important for managing your money.
- Knowing your goals and understanding the difference between wants and needs will help you tackle your spending.
- Compound interest is to your advantage when you use it for savings, but works against you when you incur debt, especially on credit cards.
- Track your spending to figure out what's mindless and can be cut.

In the next chapter, you will learn some tips for cutting back on your food expenses, both in terms of eating out and groceries.

---

[1] Emotional Intelligence: Why It Can Matter More Than IQ, by Daniel Goleman

[2] https://www.simplypsychology.org/maslow.html

[3] https://pubsonline.informs.org/doi/10.1287/mnsc.2015.2293

[4] https://www.cnbc.com/2019/10/18/minimum-amount-of-money-you-need-in-an-emergency-fund.html

[5] https://money.usnews.com/money/personal-finance/saving-and-budgeting/articles/best-expense-tracker-apps

Chapter TWO

FOCUS ON FOOD

REMEMBER the difference between wants and needs when thinking about food! You need nourishment to survive, but eating out or buying luxury items is a want. You may value the quality of your food, which means avoiding processed foods and often buying local or organic, but it's important to note that these kinds of food is more expensive than processed or fast food, which is OK. You just need to be cognizant of the trade-offs you need to make.

Cooking your own food at home is usually cheaper than going out to eat, unless you've been living on the dollar menu at the fast-food chains. However, your health is important too, and eating mainly fast food will lead to health issues down the road.

Remember to consider both nutritional value and dollar value when eating out. Much of the food in restaurants—especially in fast food and fast-casual restaurants—are loaded with calories. However, they don't provide nourishment, which is what your body really needs. This food tends to be low in the fiber, vitamins, and minerals that you would get from unprocessed foods you can cook yourself. Even in high-end restaurants, the food is often slathered in butter and cream that you don't need.

The demands of your day may require that you eat out on occasion. You can still save money and eat good food when you do so, as long as you're mindful about it. Sometimes, you may just want to treat yourself, which is OK too, as long as it's not a daily or even weekly thing.

During the coronavirus crisis, you will probably end up spending more time cooking at home anyway, so that's a bonus! While you're doing it, find fun ways to make things that you like to eat which will provide you the nourishment you need. Then, once we're able to go back to the restaurants, you'll be satisfied with going out as a treat and making the most of your meals at home. You will learn what you like to cook and master the ingredients list, which will help you cut down on grocery spending.

You may have some cookbooks lying around, and now would be a great time to pull them out and dust them off. See what looks interesting and works with what you have on hand. Whether or not you've got cookbooks, the Internet is your friend during the crisis! You can find all kinds of recipes online, and even if you are someone who prefers to watch, there are plenty of videos on preparing food too. You might end up a master onion slicer by the end of the crisis!

Quick Tips to Start Now

The following are all things you can do right this moment to save money on food. Bring this book into the kitchen with you and get going!

- **Shop your pantry**

    Most of us have a ton of things we bought because they looked interesting, or we planned to make a meal we didn't end up cooking. In other cases, something was on sale, so we ended up scooping it up but never using it. Therefore, it's a great idea to delve into the backs of your cupboard and dig out whatever's lurking back there.

    Some cans or boxes may have expiration dates. If it does and you're well past the date, toss it. Saving money is not worth getting sick! Some staples like beans can last almost for forever.

    What kind of meal can you make with these items? Depending on the variety, you might not have any idea! It's time to whip out the cookbooks. Look in the index for an ingredient to see what you can come up with, or search online for a recipe.

- **Switch to water for drinking**

    Up to 60% of the human body is actually water. Your brain and heart are both mostly composed of water, and all your other organs, including skin and bones, have water in them, which means it's crucial to stay hydrated. It's also a great way to avoid kidney stones. Your body and brain also function better when they get enough water.

    It gets even cheaper when you stop buying gallons of soda. You also don't need sugar or artificial sweetener if you drink diet soda. Artificial sweeteners play a trick on your body, and people can become addicted to the sweet taste. However, because there are no calories, your body thinks it's still hungry. That's when you start scanning the shelves (or your cupboards) for something sweet and comforting, and end up consuming more calories.

This is partially the reason why we have so many overweight people in the US; despite their use of dieting, they buy soda with no sugar or other drinks with sweeteners. It would require an entire book to explain why most diets do not work in the long term. Sweet drinks, whether sweetened with sugar or a no-calorie substitute, are a major factor. Fortunately, these sweetening agents can be easily removed, especially when you're trying to save money.

Fruit juice isn't necessary or even all that healthy for you. Packaged juice doesn't contain the natural vitamins of the fruit, and the added vitamins aren't very effective. Eat the whole fruit instead. One apple may have just a little vitamin C, but it will give you more than the juice with added vitamins.

This doesn't mean that you should go out and hoard cases of bottled water! In most cases, the water is simply bottled tap water, which is nothing special. Not only are you adding to the plastic waste that's destroying the earth and its oceans, but you're overpaying for it.

Drink tap water if you can—this means doing so unless you live in one of the handful of municipalities where the water is contaminated and unsafe to drink, such as Flint, Michigan. If you don't like the taste of your tap, buy a filter. Researchers conducted tests in which people compared bottled and tap water from unmarked glasses. Tap water finished among the top three in terms of taste almost every time.

Yes, I said to buy something! But the reality is that, over time, if you drink filtered water, it will end up being cheaper than buying sodas or bottled water. If you don't like cold water, then leave it at room temperature. Chill your water if you don't like it warm, and infuse it with fruit, lemons, or limes to add a little taste if you like.

- **Make your coffee or tea at home**

    Going out to the coffee shop may be convenient, but it is way more expensive compared to just making it at home. You don't need a specialty coffee or frappe every day.

    If you've been completely reliant on coffee shops to date, you may have to buy a coffee maker or a kettle and learn to brew the coffee yourself. Again, there's an upfront cost, but you'll end up spending less over time by making your own, which will repay your investment in a month or two. You may even already have one somewhere in your house, and now wouldn't be a bad time to pull it out from the back of the cupboard where you stashed it and dust it off.

    You can buy bags of beans at the grocery store once you go through whatever bags you already have at home. It tastes best if you buy whole beans and grind what you need just before you brew it. If you're not into that, bags of ground coffee are also fine. Just seal the bags after using to keep coffee fresh. Once you learn how to make good coffee, and our society goes back to normal, you can invite your friends over for tasting.

    If you're more of a tea fan, you can buy tea bags or loose tea and get your tea fix. I like to have a combination of caffeinated and herbal—that way, I can have a cup of herbal tea late in the afternoon for a little pick-me-up and not have to worry about whether I'll be able to sleep that night!

- **Grocery shop with a list**

    After you've gone pantry shopping, you may still need to pick up a few other items at the store, or you need to replace some food once you've cleaned out your pantry and made meals out of what you had lying around. Don't go hungry because you won't be able to control yourself! Also, don't go without a list.

Get into the habit of looking at the contents of your fridge and pantry before you go grocery shopping. Check what you have already to make sure you don't overbuy.

When you get to the grocery store, your mission is to buy *only* what's on your list. If the shelves seem to empty quickly, they will be refilled. Once the pandemic panic has passed, the shelves will quickly fill up again. Now is a good time to practice only buying what's on your list!

- Grocery shop online and pick-up at the store

    Having a hard time sticking to your list? As long as your store offers curbside pickup for free, go ahead and use that. It's especially helpful during this time of crisis, because you can stay isolated at home and avoid going into a store and coming in contact with many people all at once.

    Shop online, then go pick it up. It's easy, healthy, and less subject to temptation!

- If you need to order out, order takeout

    Ordering takeout may be a little less convenient, but delivery services are expensive, even without the tips, so avoid them whenever possible. You don't need to pay the surcharge if you can call ahead and go to the restaurant to pick your food up yourself.

- If you're sick right now...

    Some of these tips won't work if you're sick, whether you have the coronavirus or another virus, like the common cold or flu. Stay home and avoid spreading those germs if you can. If you don't have enough food from pantry shopping, then opt to get food delivered to you. Better yet, if you ask a friend, neighbor, or relative to get the food for you, so you don't have to pay the delivery charge. They can leave it at your door, so they don't get sick too.

Medium-Term Tips to Implement Within the Next Few Months

These tricks may require you to spend a little bit more time thinking about your plan. Otherwise, they may take a bit more time to implement.

- **Plan your meals at least weekly**

    Planning ahead of time means fewer nights of ordering takeout out of exhaustion and lack of food at home. It also makes grocery shopping more relaxed, because you know exactly what you need to buy for the meals you're making. It also cuts down on overbuying.

    Work around the events coming up in your life. If you have a couple nights that you know you will be working late, you may opt to buy frozen meals. They may not be that great for you, so a better idea would be to have meals prepped on, say, Sunday night, which you can then heat up easily throughout the week. If you know you have a happy hour or client lunch that week, you won't have to buy anything for those meals. Right now, you probably do need to plan on cooking them all at home!

- **DIY your food prep**

    When you go to the grocery store, it's certainly possible to buy vegetables and fruits that are already cut up into sticks or cubes for you. Many stores even have their own salad bars, which are almost comically overpriced compared to the amount of meals you could make buying the ingredients themselves. You can buy an already roasted chicken or packages of uncooked chicken pieces such as breasts, thighs, and drumsticks.

    Know that you're paying for someone else to do this prep for you. Buying a bunch of whole carrots will provide you with much more carrot for your buck than investing in a little container of carrot sticks.

Instead of paying someone to do the prep for you, cut both your costs and your vegetables. If you know you've got a busy week ahead, prep the food when you get home from the store. Prepping your food will entail slicing your carrots and peppers, washing your salad greens if you have a salad spinner, etc.

The most economic way to get chicken is to buy a whole one and roast it. You can portion out the meat and save the bones for stock. Make sure to use up the whole chicken. It's more flavorful when you cook it with the bones in instead of unwrapping a plastic-wrapped, pale chicken breast that's had the skin and bones removed.

- **Buy in bulk when you can**

    Not everything can be bought in bulk—fresh vegetables, for example, go bad pretty quickly! However, pantry staples like beans, canned tomatoes, pasta, and rice can be kept more or less indefinitely.

    When you have perishable items or those that go bad fairly quickly after opening, consider whether you can freeze what you're not using. For example, when meat is on sale at the grocery store, portion it out and freeze the extra for later. But remember—any unfrozen food cannot be frozen again, but must be consumed quickly.

- **Eating out? Go to happy hour**

    Right now during the coronavirus crisis, you may not be doing a lot of eating out, other than takeout. Reducing the number of meals you have away from home will be great for your wallet! However, there may be times when you can't convince everyone to potluck and bring their own drinks to your house. Otherwise, you may need a little bit of a treat after work.

Hit up happy hour (or lunch) rather than dinner. Both choices are almost always less expensive compared to dinner, and you may not necessarily be in the mood for the massive dinner portions that many restaurants tend to serve during those hours. Happy hour is often more fun within a more relaxed setting.

- **Eating out? Order appetizers or share entrees**

In some cases, you may not be able to make it to happy hour, or the people you're dining with insist on a more formal meal. Despite these changes in the plan, you still don't have to pay an arm and a leg to have a nice dinner. Appetizers give you a chance to try something new with smaller portions. Often, choosing two appetizers for dinner will still cost you less than having a single entree. Another option when eating with a friend is to share an entree. Most restaurant portions are quite a bit larger than you would really need, and sharing is a great way to fix that.

Either way, if you don't finish all the food, box it up to go. If it's not enough for a full portion, you can still pair the food with a little something you have at home for lunch the next day. If it's protein, make a salad to accompany it, and if it's vegetables, throw an egg on top. Get creative and don't let anything go to waste.

- **Watch the booze**

Alcohol is an enormous moneymaker for restaurants, and the markup is insane for wine and spirits. Wine by the glass is almost always a hefty surcharge, compared to buying a bottle at the wine store. You could try going to a place where you can bring your own, though some charge a "corkage fee" to open it for you.

If you plan to drink while you're out, be smart and wallet-wise about it. Have a glass of water in between each alcoholic drink, which can help prevent you from getting drunk too quickly. It will also cut down on the amount of overpriced booze you're drinking, ultimately reducing your costs.

Long-Term Planning

What does saving money mean when you're looking out for the long term? After the crisis is over, we will be able to sit and enjoy restaurants again. Hopefully, you can use this time now to develop good habits of cooking at home and save when eating out for treats and special occasions.

- **Develop a menu of the dishes you'll cook and rotate them**

    If you don't need a lot of variety in your food, this tip will work exceptionally well for you. If you do need variety, you will need a larger menu of items, including for breakfast, lunch, and dinner. You don't have to make dinner a big meal or production, so you may choose to use the same recipes for both lunch and dinner, though not on the same day.

    When at home cooking because you can't go out, you gain the opportunity to try different meals. Some may not be worth the effort (or clean-up) that you would have to put in, whereas others might be quick and terrific. Find the ones you like to make and eat, then you can rotate them throughout the week. You'll know exactly the ingredients you need, and how much you need, which will keep costs down and help prevent you from buying too much.

    You do need some variety, so make sure you're not making dishes in which potatoes are the only vegetable, for example. You can incorporate plant-based foods in, if you haven't already.

Set aside non-meat times, like Meatless Mondays, since making meals from beans and other plant-based proteins will be cheaper than buying meat.

You might have different dishes that you will want to eat throughout the different seasons. Maybe you love meatloaf, but you save that for winter time and put sloppy joes in the summer rotation. In another case, you might rotate the same protein dishes all year, but switch out the vegetables and fruits according to season.

At the end of the day, it is *your* menu! *You* get to eat what's nutritious and tasty for you and your household. Don't like beets? Don't put them in your rotation. Don't like brussels sprouts? Don't use them, but do add in broccoli and/or cauliflower since they contain similar nutrients.

- **Preserve**

    During the summer, fruit trees are laden with fruit and are quite cheap! Consider learning how to preserve your summer fruits and veggies to enjoy later on in the year and to prevent waste.

    Make jellies and jams and shrubs with your fruit. You can also pickle your fruit veggies. Don't let the abundance of zucchini go to waste!

    Another option is fermented food, which is great for your gut, so consider making your own sauerkraut and kimchi. It won't be much work on your part, and you won't need any fancy starters either.

- **Shop seasonally**

    Sure, you can buy strawberries and tomatoes in December, but *ugh*! Why would you want to? Fruits and veggies that are out of season are expensive, and they don't taste very good either.

When it's spring, buy your spring produce: berries, asparagus, and peas. In the summer, go for corn, summer squash like zucchini, and citrus. In the fall, you can enjoy apples and pears, along with the start of winter squashes. These fall produce options will also carry you through winter, with some of the cold-weather lettuces.

If you're buying at the farmer's market, think about going late. The potential downside to doing so is that, if you're shopping for something specific, there may not be any left by the time you get there! However, if you're just looking for products in general and don't need anything specific, you might still find some great bargains. The farmers prefer not to haul the food back with them, so they might give you discounts at the end of the day.

Chapter Summary

- Although food is a necessity of life, you can find ways to reduce how much you're spending on it by eating more at home and buying judiciously.
- You can implement some suggestions quickly, like "shopping" your pantry, using a list when you go grocery shopping, and drinking water instead of pricey soda or fruit drinks.
- In the medium term, do your meal planning weekly and manage costs of eating out by going out for happy hour or splitting entrees.
- Long-term steps include creating a menu of dishes that you would rotate and shopping seasonally.
- You can save several thousands of dollars a year just by managing your food.

In the next chapter, we will go over how you can reduce your household costs, such as in utilities and rent.

DANA WISE

Chapter THREE

PANDEMIC-PROOF YOUR HOME COSTS

WE tend to think of housing costs as fixed costs: the mortgage or rent is a certain amount, and the utilities are what they are. However, there are several methods that you can use right now to drop these supposedly fixed costs. Housing is a big-ticket item, and if you can reduce these costs using the tips provided below, you'll end up saving a lot of money. In the short term, there are smaller changes you can make that can really add up once you start implementing them (remember that the $20 you're saving is the equivalent to your having to earn over $6,100!)

Quick Tips to Start Now

- Adjust your thermostats to use less energy

    Did you know that you don't have to set your thermostat so that you're perfectly comfortable in a t-shirt and shorts (or sweatshirt and sweatpants), no matter the weather outside? By letting your home be a little warmer in the summer and a little cooler in the winter, you can save quite a bit of money.

The US Department of Energy estimates that nearly half of your home energy consumption is due to heating and cooling costs (Crank, 2018)[6] You will see that reducing these costs right away will make a big difference in your savings. Adjusting just 1° over eight hours can save you 1% on your bills. Multiply that by multiple degrees during the day and watch those savings grow.

In the winter, when you decrease the temperature at which your heat comes on, you can wear sweaters, sweatshirts, or warm robes so you stay warm, even when your heat hasn't come on yet. If you have ceiling fans, you can actually use those to help heat the rooms. Flip the switch so the blades rotate in a different direction, and the fan will push the warmer air at the top of the room down toward where you are.

In the summer, you'll need to flip the switch back, so the fan can once again provide a cooling breeze. Doing so will allow you to avoid turning your air conditioning (a/c) on. You might also want to try turning your desk and floor fans on to cool you off. Your location will determine whether your heating or your a/c system will be more expensive for you to run; however, you can reduce costs for both.

- **Refinance your mortgage and bank wisely**

  Now, while interest rates are low, may be a great time for you to consider refinancing your mortgage, especially if you've been able to increase the amount of equity in your home. It's definitely worth it to reach out to your mortgage professional. They may not be working in their offices during the pandemic, but most mortgage-related documentation is now done digitally, so you may still be able to contact them. Find out how much you can save on your monthly payment now, though beware of closing costs and points. However, do not spend all your cash and keep that emergency fund we described in chapter 10.

You'll definitely want to have your rational thinking hat on when comparing the numbers and deciding if—after all the costs and fees—it makes sense. You might be able to squeeze out some extra points in your benefit if the mortgage companies are looking to do some business during this cash crunch time.

This will be the same with your banking, and you might need to do a little research to figure out how much you can save while banking. However, sheltering in place will be the perfect time to do it. You may find banks that are offering discounts on fees or reducing other costs during the coronavirus pandemic—use them! These advantages and benefits will probably not be offered once the coronavirus is back under control, so don't delay. They will not stick around for long.

- **Using the dishwasher vs. hand washing dishes**

    It's actually more energy efficient to use your dishwasher compared to hand washing dishes; that is, if you have a newer model washer. If your model was built before 2013, and especially if it's pre-2000, you may be better off continuing your hand washing (Bradford, 2017).[7]

    It may seem counter-intuitive because the dishwasher uses electricity; however, you may not realize that hand washing does too because using the sink also means using your hot-water heater. Newer dishwashers heat water more efficiently than your hot-water heater does, which helps to save energy on a full load of dishes.

    Many people don't pay for water usage, but newer dishwashers are much more efficient with water than you would be washing in the sink. With hand washing, you may use up to 27 gallons washing the same load of dishes it would take your dishwasher to clean with about 3 gallons, which is a *massive* difference. If you don't pay for water, consider how much you're saving the earth too!

There are also ways to make your dishwasher even more efficient, and running full loads is one of them. Use vinegar for the rinse, then cut back on energy use by letting dishes air dry instead of using the heat dry option. If there is excess food on the plate, scrape it into the trash or compost and don't rinse before you put it in.

- **Shop home insurance and consider bundling**

    How much is your premium for home or renter's insurance? This is another bill that can be pretty hefty! While you're at home, go online or call different insurance agencies to see if you can get a better deal.

    Calling is often a great way to get a better deal because human agents are much more susceptible to your threats of leaving if they can't give you that better deal! Also, consider if you're better off bundling your car insurance. Many insurance companies will give you a better deal if you combine your home or renter's policy with your vehicle.

    As always, remember to read the fine print carefully and make sure you're not accepting reduced coverage in an effort to reduce your costs. Also, ensure any trade-offs you're making are worth it—you may get a lower monthly payment in exchange for a higher deductible, which means you would be paying more out of pocket if an incident does occur. If you can't come up with the higher deductible amount, you may need to accept a higher monthly payment.

Medium-Term Tips to Implement Within the Next Few Months

As you can see, there are plenty of ways that you can reduce the costs you may have previously thought were fixed. You can do the ones we discussed above right away. However, those aren't the only tips I'm offering. In the next few months, even after you've adjusted your thermostats and taken advantage of the short-term cuts, you can still continue to drive your home costs down.

- **Choose energy-efficient products when it's time to replace**

    When you're renting, some landlords will provide things like refrigerators and washing machines, but there are many who don't. In these cases, you may also need to replace a microwave or other small appliances. If you're a homeowner, you'll definitely need to replace these items over time, in addition to larger expenses like roofs, windows and doors.

    As stated, appliances and other household items wear out over time and will need to be replaced. Some last longer than others, but it's likely that you will have to buy new things after a while. When you're replacing all these items, you don't need the most expensive or flashiest new model; for example, if you're a household of two people, there's no reason to buy a washing machine that can handle loads for a household of six. Match the appliance to your own usage.

    The other important factor in replacement is its energy efficiency. If you have an older model and think it may have another year in it, research perks that would come from newer models. If you've got something that's ten years old or older, the newer models will likely save you a lot more money just through energy efficiency. For example, replacing your old washing machine with a newer model that uses half energy and half water can save you a lot over the next year.

Your home's insulation can make a huge difference in your heating and cooling costs. If your weatherstripping is old or nonexistent, you may be losing a lot of energy to the great outdoors. Make sure that your replacement doors and windows are energy efficient.

If you live in a hotter climate, your window dressing can actually save you money as well. Mini blinds can't do much for you, but you can buy sunlight-blocking sheers and blackout curtains to darken the room. They are great for sleeping and saving money on a/c when the sun can't heat the room as well.

- **Do housework for the landlord in exchange for rent reduction**

    There is a lot of work that goes into keeping up a property. Landlords need to keep their place looking nice to attract good tenants. With all the upkeep required, you may be able to make a tradeoff for them, so they don't have to spend money on gardeners or exterior painters.

    If there's a laundry room or other common area, it needs to be kept clean. See if your cleaning abilities can help with your rent! Either way, you can at least try this tactic to avoid a rent increase.

- **Save money with lights**

    If it's hard to remember to turn the lights off when you've finished your business in a room, it may be a good idea to install occupancy sensors. Infrared sensors work on heat and motion and turn the lights on when someone's in the room. They will also turn them off when they no longer detect heat or movement. Outside, motion-activated lights will work well on your front door and elsewhere, placed strategically for your protection.

    You can also consider dimming your lights, which would save you energy and make your modern light bulbs last longer. Dim lights require less energy, and dimmers are great for rooms or hallways that you don't use all the time, but where you might need some light at night. Dimming doesn't work as well for old-school incandescent use, as it shortens their typical lifespan.

Both LED and compact fluorescents (CFLs) are more energy efficient than incandescent bulbs. You'll want to make sure you choose the right color LED for the room. Those on the lower end of the light spectrum create a warmer, cozier light, whereas those at the higher end are clearer and brighter. High spectrum lights are well suited for task or office lighting, though you may want a cozier, warmer glow in the bedroom.

o Use smart power strips

When items like computers and televisions are plugged in, they consume a little energy even while turned off. Smart power strips manage the electricity that goes to each outlet on the strip to maximize energy efficiency, and all might shut off if there's no activity on the strip for a while.

When the main item is shut off, all the others associated with it would also be shut off. For example, suppose you have a television set with a game console, streaming stick, and soundbar associated with it. When you shut off the TV with a smart strip, the console, stick, and bar shut down too. For your wifi router, there may be an "always on" socket.

o Consider housemates or short-term rentals

As noted above, rent and mortgage are significant expenses. You can slash them along with utility bills by sharing the cost with someone else. If you have an unused room, think about renting it out to a housemate or for short-term rental.

Although you may feel a bit nervous at sharing your place long-term, it seems unlikely that short-term rentals will bounce back right away after the coronavirus crisis has ended. Many people haven't been able to work, so vacation plans will probably be put on hold in the future.

By the same token, plenty of people will probably need to cut back on expenses whenever they can, just like you. Just as a side, it will likely be easier to find a roommate than it will be to find someone to rent for the short term. Be active, look around, and post on social media.

Make sure you know what your landlord or housing association will accept! Protect yourself legally in case you run into a problem with your roommate not paying, which may mean they will have to be put on the lease so the landlord can evict them. That protection will also assure your association or town won't fine you for short-term rentals.

- **Reduce, reuse, recycle, upcycle**

  While it's true that energy-consuming home items and materials are most energy-efficient when they're new, that's not necessarily true for everything in your home. A brand new chair won't be more energy-efficient than your old chair, and it may be even worse for the environment, since modern manufacturing methods are known to cause damage to the earth.

  So, when it comes to furniture and dishes, for example, instead of upgrading and buying a newer version, don't be afraid to get creative. Trust me—if there's anything you want to do around the house, there will probably be a video or graphic tutorial online that will teach you how to do it!

  If you're tired of the way your chairs look, reupholster them using materials you have lying around. Try your hand at needlecrafting if you require new napkins, tablecloths, placemats, or wall hangings. You can also take an old nightstand and create a desk out of it.

Although a professional could probably do the work for you, the money going to them could be placed somewhere else instead. Professionals use new materials, and repair costs may be close to the price of a new item. If you cannot repair it properly, at least prolong its life with smaller, quick, and easy fixes.

You can reuse chipped glasses as toothbrush mugs or pencil holders. Old dishes you don't like can sit under your plants and catch the water and heavy bowls you don't like can be repurposed for feeding and watering pets. For cleaning rags, cut up, old, and stained t-shirts. They will also be good for wiping down your electronics. You can wash your rags in your energy-efficient washing machine. On the other hand, if you do need to use paper towels, challenge yourself to make that paper towel roll last as long as possible!

What do you have lying around in your cupboards or crammed into the back of your drawers? If you can't think of anything for any miscellaneous items you find, see what shows up on a quick internet search. You might be surprised.

- **Plan furniture buying ahead of time**

    When you go impulse shopping, for anything—food, clothes, and furniture, for example—you tend to spend more money than you should. In those cases, you may not even end up with something you genuinely like because you felt pressured into buying that item.

    Planning ahead of time allows you to budget and save up the amount you need. Thus, you wouldn't need to worry about having interest work against you; instead, buy it for cash or put it on a credit card for points but pay the debt off immediately.

    Thrift and consignment stores are your friend, and you may find some cheap, badly used particleboard nonsense. Chances are, you'll find some furniture with patterns that are absolutely hideous, and no one decorates their homes like the 1980s anymore for a reason. However, you'll also find furniture built out of solid materials that were made to last and consider what's underneath the hideous pattern. Is the frame well-made? You can always reupholster a nightmare fabric if it's located on a beautiful frame that was built to last.

Giving yourself time to buy also means you can spend some time looking. You may also be able to strike a deal, particularly in a thrift store where the owner needs space for new stuff regularly.

Long-term planning

Even more money can be saved over the long term with planning and questioning. Many of us tend to stick with decisions once we've made them, even as circumstances change; however, what was the best for us and our families five years ago may no longer be the optimal choice. Now's a good time to question whether where we're living is still the right place for us and, if so, how we can make it sustainable and less expensive through the coming years.

- Smart and efficient major renovations

    Where you are right now can be a great place in terms of neighborhood and environment. You may not want to make any changes in location in the near future. However, your house itself may need some major changes to accommodate your needs. You upcycled and recycled as much as you could, but now you're looking at larger structural changes for your home.

    As with any big home project, make sure you get plenty of bids for the work and do your homework. With every major change, think about energy efficiency in your projects and how the proposed changes will affect your heating and cooling bills. If you live in a hotter climate, maybe a glass-enclosed atrium facing west isn't a great idea! Ensure that the windows you're planning will be well-insulated.

How will the roof of a new addition fit with your existing roof, and how will it handle the heat and rain? If you're opening up space indoors by taking down walls, how does that affect your HVAC and electrical systems? These are all questions you need to consider while reworking your home. Big changes can make your house feel completely new! With every renovation, make a goal to improve your energy efficiency.

- **Consider buying a fixer-upper if in the hunt for a new house**

If you're looking for a new home, you'll need to do some math if you want to get the most out of every penny. Most neighborhoods usually have a mix of older and newer homes, so you won't immediately be comparing apples to apples.

The older homes may be well-cared-for, fixer-uppers, or a mix of both. At first glance, the fixer-uppers would look the most economical, and they may very well be! However, you'll need to take the calculator out to make sure. What energy-efficient upgrades will you need to make on your chosen fixer-upper? Often, you'll need to replace the windows and, perhaps, the doors. How much work will the inside take? Even the handiest people should hire an electrician for the wiring. Don't forget to add dimmers and occupancy sensors if necessary.

Your creativity in recycling and upcycling will come in handy here. The great thing about fixer-uppers is that, when renovating, you get to make the house exactly the way you want it. Keep in mind that older homes that have been maintained better may be more expensive to start with, and you may still need to do some work to make sure they're energy-efficient. It may need a new roof, windows, and doors. When comparing with a brand new house, do your research to figure out how efficient it really is. Does it have upgraded, efficient features? It may be new, but efficiency is no guarantee!

Energy efficiency is often overlooked because people focus on the purchase price. At this point now, however, you can recognize how the overall price would also include utilities and necessary renovations. These can be strong arguments when negotiating price.

- How big a home do you really need?

Just as you don't need a washing machine that handles the filth of six people when there's only two of you in the house, it's not necessary to buy a large house when you don't plan to fill it with people.

There are many benefits to buying a house that's only as big as you need it to be, and no bigger. Smaller houses are more energy efficient. You also don't have as many rooms to heat, cool, light, and clean.

In general, they're also quite a bit cheaper upfront, at least when you're comparing houses that are in similar locations. A house out in the suburbs of a major city may appear cheaper at first compared to a smaller condo downtown in that same city. The reason it only appears so at first is because, after looking at initial costs, you would have to factor in the commute and associated costs that come with that.

- Smaller house prices may be cheaper this year (2020)

Recessions tend to depress housing markets too, though certain markets are relatively immune to stock market drops. However, home builders, recognizing the need to house millennials, are building more entry-level homes, so you might get lucky!

- **Move to a less expensive suburb**

    Some US cities are becoming too expensive to live in, so you may need to move to a suburb anyway. You will notice that certain suburbs are more affordable than others. Remember to be mindful about your purchase.

    Therefore, you don't need to move to the most chic, hipster suburb for your city. Instead, broaden your scope. Other neighborhoods may not look as cool and you might have to walk farther to the shops that you need, but if it's cheaper, you should consider it!

    The price of housing goes hand in hand with other living expenses. In higher end suburbs, you may see some of your neighbors having a higher standard of living. Your children might meet wealthier schoolmates daily, and they may find it difficult to cope with the differences. Often, we compare our lives with others unconsciously when making important decisions. If your neighbors just bought a brand new car and took an expensive vacation, how will you feel if you can't afford to do the same?

    On the other hand, a neighborhood that's less wealthy may be more supportive. You'll find more people in your community who don't measure by wealth or, more accurately, by spending. Remember what we said at the beginning—your value is not how much money you have, make, or spend! Your value is in who you are. Having like-minded people around you is better than owning the biggest house in town, or even living next door to it.

    If you're in a city with relatively affordable housing, you can start calculating the cost of your commute. If you can get there by public transportation, that should be a relatively easy number to figure out. Even better if your employer subsidizes the trip!

    If you'll be commuting by car, a good way to estimate the costs is to start with the IRS mileage reimbursement. In 2020, it is currently

57.5 cents a mile. If your commute is 20 miles each way, that's $2.13 per day, or $11.50/week and $575 per year, assuming a 2 weeks vacation (International Revenue Agency [IRS], 2020).[8]

The IRS reimbursement is essentially gas and regular wear and tear. It doesn't include the cost of repairs or insurance, so make sure your total commute cost adds those in. Compare the cost of the suburban house, including gas or transit costs and time, with the house in the city to make sure you are making the most cost-effective decision.

- Add awnings, shade trees, and ceiling fans

    These additions will help cool your house down in the summer. You may want awnings over your doors in addition to your windows; however, depending on the direction your house faces, you may not need awnings on all your windows. Focus on the ones that catch most of the sun's heat during the day.

    While doing your landscaping, think about how large the trees will grow and if you have the right soil for them. Also, think about how long it will take for them to reach full height! You may not have the time to wait for a slow-growing tree to protect your west-facing windows. Though the tree may not be huge at first, make sure it has room to grow away from the house, accounting for root space. A large tree can grow to be quite some distance from the house and still provide enough shade in the summer.

    Earlier in the chapter, we mentioned using existing ceiling fans to cool off or heat up the room. If you don't have fans, consider installing them. You can leave your a/c set at a much higher temperature at night when you're cooled by a fan right above the bed.

- Preventative maintenance

    Once you've renovated or found your wonderful home, keep it that way. Keep the paint fresh so water doesn't start seeping into the house through cracks, and if your climate is friendly to mold and mildew, make sure you tend to susceptible areas regularly. Live in a dry climate? Use a humidifier.

Always repair foundation cracks. Clear out your gutters and downspouts, and angle the downspouts away from your basement and foundation. If you take care of the small issues, they won't snowball into bigger ones or reduce the efficiency you worked so hard to create.

Chapter Summary

- Your home is a big-ticket item, and there are a number of ways to reduce the costs associated with it, though they may at first appear to be fixed.
- You can shop for better insurance rates, adjust your thermostat, and refinance your mortgage all immediately.
- In the medium term, consider renting out a room, replacing older appliance models for energy-efficient new ones, planning big furniture buys, and reusing and recycling things you already own.
- In the long term, consider whether your living arrangement is the best and most economical option for you at this time, and see what will be the best investment for you should you decide to move.
- When deciding to move, consider the neighborhood and whether it will fit your lifestyle.

In the next chapter, we will be discussing how to reduce your spending on electronics and devices.

---

[6] https://www.directenergy.com/blog/how-much-can-you-save-by-adjusting-your-thermostat/

[7] https://www.cnet.com/how-to/how-much-water-do-dishwashers-use/

[8] https://www.irs.gov/tax-professionals/standard-mileage-rates

Chapter FOUR

WIRED FOR SMART BUDGETING

IN the introduction, we talked about how some necessities of modern life, like cellphones and the internet, would have been unimaginable to your great-grandparents. Some of us tend to think of these as fixed costs too as a result, but they aren't.

Many of the devices themselves are similar; however, you may needlessly spend more money on one brand compared to another. There's absolutely no reason to stick with one brand out of loyalty or popularity. Save money by buying the device that will work just as well while costing you less because now is not the time to try to signal your belonging in a "club" and paying more than you need. The same goes for service providers.

There are plenty of ways to get what you want without overpaying, and you may not have been aware that they're out there. Therefore, I have rounded them up for you. Knowledge is power! So, go forth and save with this information.

Quick Tips to Start Now

As with most of the suggestions in this book, having to sit at home during the coronavirus means it's a great time to start implementing the following tips. You will get to be productive when you implement these changes, especially if you aren't working during this time.

- **Call for discounts on phone/Internet access**

    We mentioned this point briefly in the last chapter when discussing home and renter's insurance. Beyond material items, phone and Internet companies are even more notorious for dropping your monthly bill to keep you. You may want to jump on this fact as soon as possible when prices are so low too. Note that if you qualify for some kind of hardship assistance, you should absolutely take advantage of that too.

    It's much cheaper for them to keep you than to add a new customer, and the prices are essentially arbitrary anyway; it doesn't cost them $75 a month to keep the internet flowing into your Wi-Fi. Call and let them know you're ready to walk unless they can give you a better price.

    All service providers offer teaser rates for new clients, so it's not an empty threat on your part. This is true for most people, unless you live in a remote area with only one provider. In that case, you should still call and see if they can drop your rates. What's the worst that could happen? They'll say no. Nothing ventured, nothing gained.

- **Get rid of excess services you don't need on your cell phone, like call waiting**

    Many people barely use their phones for its original design, which was voice communication. If that's you, you definitely don't need any extra voice services. Along with that, drop anything else you don't need from your plan.

- **Drop the landline if you have one**

  Now that cell phones have become pretty popular, you probably no longer need a landline. Your phone has GPS, so emergency services can still locate you quickly. Also, if you have an accident in your home, it's more likely that your mobile phone is closer to you than your landline anyway. At this point, for the vast majority of people, a landline is a completely unnecessary expense, so let it go.

- **Mobile phone alternatives**

  Once you've called your phone company and threatened to leave if you didn't get a lower rate, that's the best you can do, right?

  Wrong! At least for many.

  Most monthly service plans cost a certain amount depending on how much you think you'll use your data. If you use less than that, you've probably lost a lot of money. Likewise, if you use more, you may pay a surcharge or see your data throttled (slowed down).

  When considering one of the following alternatives, evaluate what your past usage has been for data—this includes streaming, checking your email, social media apps online, among other activities. Depending on your plan, that may or may not include text messaging. Check your past statements to see how much you normally use.

  Prepaid plans are often significantly cheaper than monthly service plans from the big carriers, at least when it comes to voice services. If you're a heavy data user, these plans may not work as well because they usually don't offer as many minutes on their data plans.

Another option for users who don't gobble up gobs of data is a pay-per-use service, such as Google Fi. You would only pay for the services you use, so if you don't use much data, you'll typically pay significantly less with these services.

You could also try Voice-Over-Internet-Protocol or VOIP. It's a cheaper way to talk, and it might even be a cheaper way to text! However, you won't be able to use it to watch your favorite videos or check your emails.[9]

- Ditch cable TV and/or satellite TV

    With all the entertainment available on streaming services, there's no real reason to keep paying as much as you do on cable or satellite TV. You can probably get everything you want over the Internet, in one form or another.

    In the next section, we'll be discussing streaming in more detail. For now, just cancel it. There are plenty of cheaper ways to access entertainment. I personally haven't had cable TV for over ten years. Whenever I visit my friends or relatives and there's a TV on, I constantly notice how much I save and that I'm not missing out!

    I am not allowing that stream of mostly terrible films, bad news, and advertisements to attack and influence me. That stream was prepared by somebody who does not have the same values as I do, and their only purpose is to get watchers to sit through the ads. Why should I pay for something that I don't actually want?

Medium-Term to Implement in the Next Few Months

You've canceled your cable and gained a better deal on your phone and Internet services. There are a couple more steps you can take to help you save on these services in the next few months.

- **Avoid annual phone upgrades**

    Every year, each phone company unveils their latest device with a big advertising campaign and makes it seem like it's necessary, even though it's really not. Once in a while, a manufacturer might genuinely come out with a game changer in the new version that makes upgrading worth your while. Most of the time, however, there's hardly any difference between last year's version and this year's.

    Manufacturers often want to drain as much money out of your wallet as possible, and that does not mean you have to let them. An extra pixel on the camera, or a camera in a slightly different place or with a slightly sharper bevel won't actually change your life. Save your money.

    Having said that, these devices are designed for obsolescence. After a few years, your phone may stop working and you'll need to replace it. Be smart and purchase only what you need. Right now, I'm using a seven-year-old iPhone 5, which required a replacement for the broken display, as well as the battery three times. Some newer applications that just came out can no longer be installed on it; however it still works for emails, internet, and weather forecasts, which are all that I really use. I'm quite sure it will stop working within the next year. That will be when I choose a model that meets my requirements at that time.

- **Consider the streaming services you need**

    Did you cut the cable cord easily because you're signed up for a whole bunch of streaming services? You probably don't need them all, and once you really think about it, you may realize you only need one or two. You may even realize you don't need any of them. You can probably get most of what you want on a free video platform like YouTube or Vimeo, so you can try checking those out first.

    Keep in mind that you don't need to watch the same shows that everyone else in your office is watching. Back in the day, when there were only three channels, everyone talked about what was on TV because nearly everyone watched the same stuff. There wasn't much variety. Now, however, with the explosion of cable, streaming, and even user content, everyone watches something different, and everyone's conversations completely vary in terms of television.

    If you have kids, it may make going streaming-free a bit harder. Although we can probably agree that kids shouldn't be spending as much time in front of a screen, it can really help if you work from home and need to distract them. If you are considering this change and want to start working remotely, you can find many more great tips in my book *Work from Home During and After Coronavirus*.

    Kid-friendly shows are great life-savers in this regard. Likewise, if you don't have kids, think hard about whether you really need that kid's channel. They can be quite expensive. Focus your streaming and television watching on your personal interests.

    Absolutely cannot give up streaming TV? You can first try giving it up for a month or two before declaring that is the case.

You might surprise yourself. If it is the case and you really *do* need some streaming services, then pick one that has the content you watch the most.

Long-Term Planning

There is only one major suggestion for the long term, and it's a pretty important one.

Stop spending so much time on your devices. Period. Substitute it with human contact, whether it's in-person or on the phone talking, and avoid texting or bantering on social media. Although spending time on social media seems to be the newest form of social communication, studies have found that it can actually make you feel more depressed, isolated, and less connected to others (Alyssa, n.d.).[10] Although social media most definitely has its uses and can help you connect with others, including for job-searching, so you might not want to give it up completely. Be judicious as you use it.

As shocking as it may sound, social media is the largest addiction people experience today. The apps are designed to give you a dopamine hit when you scroll over a nice image, see a message from a friend, or get a like. As with any addiction, those good feelings end quickly, so you continue scrolling to get another hit.

The apps and platforms were deliberately designed to be addictive, allowing the advertisers to show you their ads for a longer period while you scroll through your feed (Price, 2018).[11]

Social media uses your data and Wi-Fi, and the less data you're using on your devices, the cheaper your bills will be. There's no reason to pay through the nose for unlimited data when you can drop your usage significantly by lessening your time on social media. You will also end up feeling better as a result!

Chapter Summary

- While phones and Internet access are necessary for modern life, you don't have to overpay for them.
- Social distancing at home makes now a great opportunity to call for reducing monthly fees, and also to consider using a different type of service if doing so will lower your bills.
- Over the next few months, avoid needless device replacement and consider how many streaming services you really need.
- Reduce the amount of time you spend on your devices, as doing so will drop your data costs and help you reconnect.
- If you can after the pandemic, opt for in-person social connection, which will save you money and stronger social connections. Charge yourself with real social connection.

In the next chapter, we will learn all about cheap or free entertainment options that serve both your body and mind.

---

[9] https://www.genvoice.net/can-people-send-and-receive-text-messages-via-voip/
[10] https://www.bhpalmbeach.com/are-depression-and-social-media-usage-linked/
[11] https://www.sciencefocus.com/future-technology/trapped-the-secret-ways-social-media-is-built-to-be-addictive-and-what-you-can-do-to-fight-back/

DANA WISE

Chapter **FIVE**

ENTERTAINMENT THAT'S FUN AND FRUGAL

MOST of us are used to spending money on entertainment. We rent out or watch movies at the movie theater, buying buckets of popcorn, soda, and candy, along with the ticket for the film itself. We buy tickets to watch professional sports or for music concerts. Some of us have been known to use shopping as entertainment, heading to the mall to look at the stores, buy things we don't need, and eat food that isn't that nourishing. At the end of the day, many of us slump into the recliner, pick up the remote, and start flipping through channels.

We've paid one way or another for our entertainment in terms of money. Depending on your hobbies and what you enjoy watching passively, you might have paid hundreds or thousands of dollars for the privilege of inhaling what someone else has made.

Now, while you can't watch sports, go to the movies, or wander the mall aimlessly due to the pandemic restrictions, it is a terrific time to get yourself out of bad habits. You can still have plenty of fun without spending so much money. For now, we suddenly have a chance to break some habits! Replace passive activities with ones we genuinely enjoy and don't have to spend much, if any, money on.

Ready to start having an awesome time, even when staying at home? Then read on!

Quick Tips to Start Now

We have a good long list of things you can do right now while social distancing at home. Start with these suggestions, and you'll be surprised with how fast the days actually go by.

- Go outside

    This one is pretty self-explanatory. Watching TV online or through streaming and spending time on your phone are passive activities that you would usually do sitting down. However, it turns out sitting all day is actually dangerous to your health! ("Dangers of Sitting," n.d.)[12]

    Some people get confused by the shelter-in-place orders that many of us are currently living under. That doesn't mean you have to stay inside all day and never leave the house. You can definitely go out for walks, just make sure to practice social distancing and not get too close to others who might be out enjoying the sunshine with you. However, authorities in some countries have restricted going outside and to public places, which must be obeyed.

    If you have a yard, get out there with your family and pet and play around. Kids don't do well cooped up indoors, and fresh air is good for everyone. Being out in nature is a boost for both your mental and physical health.

I personally like working in my garden. I plant various vegetables and fruits and care for my fruit bushes. Do I save a lot of money with this? Maybe not. However, I do get to enjoy eating my own products, fresh from the garden. I find they have the best taste. I also have flowers, trees, and a lot of plants around the house. I could remove these beauties and have just grass to mow, but I enjoy the sun and being out in the fresh air. Plus, I don't have to worry about going to the gym because gardening will give me a good amount of exercise.

Being outside also means you're getting away from your screens. If you absolutely must bring your phone with you, don't carry it in your hand. Put it in a pocket or purse. Also, remember to pay attention to what's going on around you. What's your child or spouse saying to you? What does the sky look like? Anything new in the neighborhood? Recognizing the answers to these questions will help keep you and your loved ones safe.

- **Skype/Zoom/FaceTime friends and family**

    For most of us, being with our loved ones and close friends is not a possibility right now. Some of us have family living an entire country or more away. As discussed in the last chapter, using social media and texting may not work for everyone.

    We humans are uniquely attuned to faces, and so it's important for us to be able to see the faces of the people we're talking to (Nottingham, 2017).[13] Therefore, when we can't be with each other physically, it's important to be able to see each other when possible. Phone calls are better than texting and typing; however, being face-to-face, even if we're not geographically close to one another, is best.

- **Learn an interesting new craft or skill online**

    Fortunately, many of us have the Internet while we're all

staying home, which means, as long as you're using it correctly, you have a wealth of information at your fingertips.

It's easy to start scrolling and eventually end up down a rabbit hole! However, if you confine your search to something you're interested in while avoiding social media, you'll be OK. You may end up learning far more about your chosen subject than you thought you would.

Almost every hobby or craft that you can try is available online in the form of diagrams, blog posts, and even how-to videos. There are also discussion forums, tips and tricks articles, and "if only I'd known..." advice. A huge bonus to searching these up is that most of them are free!

No one can see you mess up or look goofy when you're in the comfort of your own home, so it's the perfect time to start learning something new. Who knows—you may have picked up a new and useful skill by the time social distancing is over.

o **Read/listen to books from the library**

Readers often like to buy books, but that can certainly get expensive. Investing in a library card would be a great option for these people because it's always free. Many local libraries are part of a larger system—for example, many US counties operate several libraries. If the one closest to you doesn't have the book you want, you can probably order it from another library in the system. Transfers are usually free too. If you don't already have a library card from your local library, you may be able to sign up online.

There are plenty of books available for reading. Some people prefer to listen, and you can download audiobooks from various sources, often for free. You may be able to download free ebooks from your library as well. Plus, just as with audiobooks, there are a number of sources that are either free or reasonably cheap.

Novels help you empathize with other people by allowing you to step into the minds of the characters. If you're having trouble understanding why other people are having such a hard time with isolation, reading a novel may be a great idea for you!

There is a lot of information on the Internet, but the vast majority of it is in bite-size pieces. That information is also often redundant from post to post. Books, however, can provide a much deeper dive into the subject you're interested in.

- **No browsing or putting items in your online cart - buy nothing**

  Break the habit of online shopping. As of the writing of this book (March 2020), the major product shippers are sending out priority items such as cleaning supplies first. In other words, now is an excellent time to practice not shopping. If you don't need anything, stop browsing.

  It can be easy to get mesmerized by the advertising in front of you on the screen. Remember—these platforms are designed to capture you so the advertisers can get their content in front of you. Admen and women have been in the game of influencing you for decades, and the easiest way to avoid losing the game is to refuse to play it in the first place.

  Don't bother with deal sites either, unless you need something specific. Disable the notifications or unsubscribe from their emails, as the only thing you will miss out on is having your wallet drained.

  Challenge yourself to buy nothing except for the necessities like groceries and cleaning supplies for a few months. If you run out of something and need to replace it, you can do that. However, you should check whether you really need to replace it before you do.

- **If you must add to your cart, don't click "buy" right away**

    Sometimes, old habits die hard. Before you go online shopping, however, disable one-click or anything else that makes buying online instant. You want it to be hard and forcing you to think about it because, the more rational you are about it, the less you'll actually purchase.

    If you do put something in the cart, leave it for a few hours. Advertisements telling you to come back and buy will pop up automatically due to the site's algorithms, but you need to resist. You might see a price pop up that claims you'll only get the special price if you buy now.

    Marketers aim for your emotions. They play on your fear of losing a special discount or missing something important if you don't buy now because they know that, if you take the time to consider whether you need a product, you probably won't buy it. Thus, you are faced with the "buy now with a discount" techniques. Remember—they don't care about you and don't have your best interests in mind. They have their own profit motive in mind, which may or may not align with your values. Most of the time, it doesn't.

    No one on the other side of the screen is desperate for you to buy! There's an automated algorithm that has been programmed to ask you these questions before you leave the site. The algorithm analyzes your behavior and uses cookies on your computer to discover a lot about you. It then directs the conversation specifically to people similar to you: women, young adults, or people living in certain regions. Advertisers know precise questions increase the purchase rate, so don't let them game you.

    Likewise, consider buying from Chinese companies such as Aliexpress or Wish. The price is usually a fraction compared to the US stores online and, depending on the product, you could find the same items 60-90% cheaper. Many US stores may sell exactly the same product, but nicely packed and with a brand attached. Despite the cheaper cost, delivery time may be longer, and it can take weeks due to shipment time from China, custom clearance, and transfer between several shippers. Therefore, make note that just because it only costs $1 doesn't mean you have to buy it instantly. Add in the cost of shipping—US online companies may also offer free delivery and discounts for Black Friday or Cyber Monday. Be wise and compare product pricing overall.

Medium-Term to Implement in the Next Few Months

Once things have calmed down—whatever that may look like—there will be time and opportunity to get together with friends and family. That means sharing and connecting, which are both important to human beings.

Rather than watching TV or sports, try joining a recreational sports league, going for a walk, or hanging out with your friends. Such will satisfy the human need for connection, along with your body's need for activity to stave off inflammatory diseases like cardiovascular disease, Type II diabetes, and certain cancers. It also protects your brain from neurodegenerative diseases, such as Alzheimer's and dementia.

- **Hang out with friends at the local park or each other's houses instead of hitting the bars**

    You might be hanging out with your friends over Skype right now, but that will probably change at some point. Don't stop being with friends now that you can be geographically close to them!

    Going to the bar with friends does allow you to stay connected; however, it also allows you to spend a lot of money that you don't need to spend and doesn't provide you with much mental or physical stimulation.

Try to do two things at once when making time with your friends, if you can. For example, you can go to the park with your friends, effectively satisfying your needs for human connection and for nature at the same time. It's hard to sit still on a beautiful day, so you may as well get some movement in as well.

Rather than going to the bar having overpriced drinks, go to your house or your friend's house with your own drinks. Doing so will save you a ton of money. Play games, have fun, and exercise your brain a little.

- **Become an artist**

    There's no reason that you always have to read someone else's story, watch their movie, or listen to their music. You can try picking up the instrument that you played as a kid. You may have lost the ability to read music by this point, but that's what online tutorials are for!

    Many people experience the deep human need to create. Why are you watching someone else's show? Write your own story, make your own movie, and film yourself doing a silly dance or creating something interesting. There's no reason you have to settle for someone else's when making your own is great for your brain (Stahl, 2018).[14]

    When you get together with people with whom you share common interests, you'll also be connecting and socializing. Just like with close friends, all this art making and befriending can take place at someone's house or the park; therefore, there is no need to rent out a pricey studio or go to a fancy bar. After joining a community with people who share your interests, you will often receive great understanding, support, and encouragement from them.

- **Potluck dinners with friends and colleagues**

    Some people really enjoy eating different foods while not cleaning up after themselves after every meal! However, going out to eat constantly can become pretty expensive. Even if you only venture to a cafe or bistro—both of which tend to be cheaper than a fine dining restaurant—you're still spending money you don't really need to.

    Instead, you can agree to potluck at someone's house over a set number of times each week or month. Who brings what rotates between you, along with who hosts. You can create themes and work around food sensitivities, all the while eating great food that others have cooked. You may have to clean when it's your turn to host, but you will still be saving more money than if you went out to eat over the same frequency.

    Some people formalize this into a supper or dinner club. You can do that too, if you prefer the feel of a more luxurious treat. However, you can also stay with the coziness and informality of potluck. It's a great way to get to know people you work with on a deeper level, so, without formally networking, you will still be networking. It's also a great way to get to know your neighbors if you decide to start one in your neighborhood.

- **Amateur sports games instead of professional ones**

    If you really want to go watch some sports instead of playing them, consider your local leagues instead. Major pro sports tickets are incredibly expensive, and the games are held pretty far from home for many people; therefore, you also need to factor in the cost of getting there and back.

    Don't forget all the money you would probably spend on food and memorabilia at a pro sports arena. Many people feel the need to memorialize their trip with some kind of souvenir.

Thus, are you going to the game because you love the sport, the players, or do you love to spend money? If it's the sport, you could probably go watch the local teams play instead for far less money or for free. They're less likely to be selling expensive souvenirs, in addition to much cheaper tickets. The hot dog and soda is probably more reasonably priced than it is at the fancy stadium. In some cases, you might not even be hungry because you haven't had to make a day of it. The money you do spend at amateur games would also probably support the local club or kids learning the sport.

You're more likely to see friends and colleagues at a local game than across a crowded arena that seats thousands. When you really think about it, there are a lot of reasons to go watch local games in your area!

- **Beyond just watching sports, go try them out yourself**

    To take the above argument even farther, if you really love the sport, you could also try playing it. Therefore, get out there on the field and give it your all. You can join a rec or amateur league in whatever sport you desire, and some sports—like swimming—have a Masters level for swimmers who are past college age, and you can join one of those teams. Your local YMCA or gym probably has some adult sports teams too. You can pick your level and have at it.

    The main reason to join a team is not necessarily to be the best in the league, but to go out, have fun, and get a bit of exercise too. You can even see if your neighbors or colleagues want to play a sport with you. Many large companies support their employees organizing sports teams, games, or running together in the local race.

    If you have injuries, you'll need to be careful. In most cases, you won't be alone, and you may still be able to find a sport or league that caters to people who can't move as fast or throw as hard, depending on your injury. For example, you may be unable to play tackle football anymore, but flag football with close friends might be perfect for you. In addition, there are plenty of physical activities you can do at any age, like archery.

- **Go to the matinee if attending a symphony/the theater**

    Most artistic institutions have both expensive and cheaper performances. No matter what it is, matinees are always cheaper and are usually held in the early afternoon. Theaters will often run performances from Friday to Sunday, and the least expensive ticket is the Sunday afternoon matinee, so grab it!

    Movie theaters will often discount the early movie times—before noon—quite cheaply. Otherwise, they may have special days where tickets are cheaper, such as Tuesdays, when they don't often have a lot of attendees.

- **Go to free days at the museums and other attractions**

    The vast majority of museums and other attractions have time during the week when entrance is free. In some lucky cases, entrance is free all the time, like the Smithsonian in Washington, DC or the zoo in St. Louis, MO. These attractions and the days they are free may not be as convenient, and they most likely won't be. Just as movie theaters pick Tuesday for their discount day because that's when people rarely go to the movies, these attractions will pick a time when they don't typically get many visitors. Depending on the size of the attraction and its location, you may be able to go several times in one month and see something different!

    Not all museums are for children, even though many people think they are. Some are designed for children, so you should absolutely take your kids there, especially on the free days.

However, as an adult, you shouldn't be at all worried about going in just because of others' perceptions. Chances are, if there aren't any large museums nearby, there will be a small historical society or art museum that you can check out from time to time.

Otherwise, your community may have other attractions with free days. If you're not sure, check online or look up your local chamber of commerce for tourist information. Either one will let you know what's free and when.

- **Go to the park**

    Most parks are free, though you may need a pass for certain national parks. Local parks often have picnic areas, basketball or tennis courts, and paths to hike. They're a great way to get active in the fresh air. Parks become even better when you visit them with friends.

- **Look at discounts you qualify for at parks, movies, etc.**

    You may be affiliated with a company or an organization that provides discounts for attractions like amusement parks, movie theaters, and even live theater performances. Large companies often donate money to their communities as part of their philanthropic efforts, and you might be able to take advantage of that as an employee. Likewise, you might be part of an organization—AAA, for example—that provides its members with discounts to various places. Your credit card company may give you discounts as part of its rewards program, so go online to see what's available to you.

    If you go to an attraction frequently, you could even consider a membership with them instead. Think about how many times you attended this place over the course of the year and how much the tickets are. If the cost turns out to be more than that of an annual membership, you should probably become a member. You'll often get some additional free perks as well.

However, only become a member after you've been there and know you'll go back. Don't be like the people who make a New Year's resolution and buy a gym membership, then never go again after January.

Long-Term Planning

By now, you should have a pretty long list of ideas that will keep you happy and occupied without having to spend a lot of money. There are more, too, when looking out toward the long term. How do you stay connected and entertained for little money when you're busy and earning money again? By then, the need to save may not feel quite so urgent.

Do what you enjoy and what feels good for you. By then, you'll have built up a habit of creativity and recycling or reusing instead of buying something new. For example, you may want to jam on instruments with your friends instead of merely listening to a playlist.

- **Join a group devoted to your hobby**

    While at home during the coronavirus pandemic, you're probably trying out a few new hobbies, such as an instrument or craft. In the early stages, you may not really know what you're doing and are a bit worried about making a fool of yourself.

    Once the awkwardness has passed, however, you'll then have some experience under your belt. Though you may not be the best one in your group if you join one, who really cares? Just have fun. Joining a group of people with similar interests is a great way to connect when trying to improve or complete a new project.

You can find groups by looking through sites such as Meetup or Eventbrite online, and you can even check a journal or web forum on your craft. Go to physical meetings if you can because those will usually be better ways to get to know people. However, if the groups are all far away from you, online is better than no group at all.

These groups will be free most of the time, especially when online. If you can't find a free group but know of some like-minded people in your area, you can organize one yourself. You can meet at the park, a local coffee shop, or in your own home. You are the organizer, so you will get to choose what works best for you.

- Go to local festivals and events

    Destination concerts and festivals have been popular since Woodstock in the 1960s. Now, depending on your taste in music and fests, you might be looking to hit a Renaissance Faire, Coachella, Stagecoach, or Electric Daisy Carnival, to name a few.

    Most of these places are pretty pricey across the board, and you will probably have to buy pretty much everything there, including water, food, and souvenirs. There is also the general cost of the festival, none of which are cheap. Add in accommodation and travel costs, and you're looking at a huge expense.

    Instead of planning a destination trip, scout around to see what's near you. If it's all about the music, there's probably a nearby spot hosting a festival. Maybe you only need a day pass. Many communities also have their own Renaissance festivals, concerts, and various holiday attractions. Save some money by going local.

- **Make your own activity**

    If you're a bit more ambitious and you have friends who are into it, why not stage your own concert lineup? Check out venues around town that are friendly to local bands, and let all your friends know on social media. You can also create shareable invites for friends to send to their friends. Then, you and your buddies can all jam out together and have a lot of fun!

    People like to see what's going on locally. Depending on how much work you want to do in advance, you might even get local businesses to sponsor. They get their names in front of your audience, and you receive some money to defray expenses.

    Another option is to make your own weekend RenFest or holiday event. It probably won't be the next Coachella, but it will at least be fun.

- **Volunteer at interesting places/events**

    One of the best ways to get into an event or place for free is to volunteer. If you love classical music but don't want to pay for the tickets, you can volunteer to usher. At the historical society, you could maybe sign up to be a guide, or you could be a tour guide at your favorite local museum. Love being around animals? Volunteer at your local animal shelter.

    Whatever your interest is, you'll probably find plenty of opportunities to volunteer. They'll normally provide you with some training, so don't worry about not being an expert when you start. Also, when you're volunteering, you're at the service of other people, which can make the brain pretty happy.

Chapter Summary

- You don't have to spend a lot of money—or any money at all—to entertain yourself once you get creative with how you want to spend your time.
- Now is the perfect time to break yourself from spending and mindless browsing habits and learn something new because you can do so in private.
- Once the restrictions have been lifted, you can hang out with your friends for free or cheap by joining recreational teams. Doing so allows you to play the sports you enjoy watching.
- After a while and once you've learned your new skill, you can be more confident in joining groups devoted to it and even consider making your own local festival or concert.
- By saving money on entertainment and getting creative about how you have fun, you're also improving your health both mentally and physically.

In the next chapter, we will go over how to reduce the costs of owning and renting vehicles.

---

[12] https://www.betterhealth.vic.gov.au/health/healthyliving/the-dangers-of-sitting

[13] https://wistia.com/learn/marketing/power-of-faces-in-video

[14] https://www.forbes.com/sites/ashleystahl/2018/07/25/heres-how-creativity-actually-improves-your-health/#18d6ba0913a6

DANA WISE

Chapter SIX

REVISIT YOUR VEHICLES

IN a car-centric country, it's easy to assume that every person of driving age needs at least one car; in some cases, they may prefer a motorcycle or a boat. Due to what appears to be cheap leases, many drivers trade up to a new vehicle every couple of years when the lease is up. Unfortunately, every vehicle—with the exception of vintage ones—is a depreciating asset, thus the value of the car dives the instant you roll it off the lot.

When reconsidering your spending plan, take a look at your fleet and see if there's anything you want to change. We have some tips for reducing various costs on your vehicles too, but getting rid of a vehicle you don't need will be the biggest moneysaver.

Quick Tips to Start Now

There are a few things that you can do right now that don't require a lot of thought. Nevertheless, they will still save you money.

- **Vehicle you don't need, like a boat? Sell it.**

  There's a saying that the two best days for a boat owner are the day they buy it and the day they sell it. Most boats are money sinks, as they require a lot of maintenance and storage space if you don't live in an area where you can leave it in the water year-round.

  If you spend a lot of time on or live in it, you may not want to sell it. However, if you rarely get a chance to sail it, even during the perfect season, you should consider selling it. You may not get back what you put into it, but it will give you some money back. On the bright side, you can then avoid maintenance and storage costs.

  Love boats? You can still rent one, as most marinas have a boat rental program.

  If it's not a boat, you may have a motorcycle or other vehicle you don't use often. Though bikes don't require as much maintenance, if you rarely ride it, it could be worth selling.

- **Shop insurance**

  If you didn't already bundle your home and car together when you reviewed the suggestions in the home chapter, you can do it now. There are a lot of insurance companies out there, so if you threaten to leave about your car insurance this time, it'll be credible.

  The company knows you have options. Just like all the mobile phone services, insurance companies find it much easier and cheaper to hang on to their current customers and would rather drop the price a bit for you than spend the money to replace you as a customer. Also, don't forget that, even if you lease a car, you're still required to maintain insurance on it.

Note that older cars aren't really worth that much due to depreciation. It doesn't stop the minute you roll off the lot, but continues throughout the life of your car. Collision coverage replaces or repairs your car if you're at fault in an accident, and comprehensive covers things like vandalism, theft, and animal collisions. If you have an older car, reduce your costs by dropping collision and comprehensive coverage. Don't ever drop your liability!

Once your car is at the point where you wouldn't make a major repair—like replacing the transmission—or 10% of the premium is more than you'd receive for a payout, you should consider selling it for parts. Wear the car out, then use the money you saved from no longer paying those premiums to get a new one.

- **Defensive (and inexpensive) driving**

   There is a saying "to drive like one's grandma," and although it may annoy some readers to hear, driving "like your grandma" will actually really help with your gas mileage and reduce the overall cost of your gas. These tips are also good for defensive driving, so you'll be able to avoid more accidents too.

   Stay a reasonable distance behind the car in front of you by obeying the 3-second rule, which will help you avoid sudden accidents. Count three seconds from a stationary item (like a light pole) when the car ahead of you passes by. If you pass it before you finish counting, you're probably too close, so drop back slightly. The faster you go, the more distance you need between you and that car. Slamming on the brakes, stomping on the gas, and speeding are all bad for your gas mileage. It depends on the car, but the miles per gallon (MPG) starts decreasing around 50 miles per hour in many vehicles (US Department of Energy [USDE], 2013).[15] In addition to avoiding unnecessary gas and break use, do your best to avoid weaving in and out of traffic and cutting people off. Doing so is rude and terrible on your gas mileage.

If applicable, take out/off excess weight and your roof rack. The rack reduces the aerodynamics of your car, and having too much in your car can also decrease your gas mileage. Reducing the amount you carry also makes you less of a target for thieves because there will be nothing for them to steal.

Idling uses a lot of gas, especially if you have the a/c on, so you're better off turning the car off instead.

When you're on the highway, use cruise control. The car's computer is much more accurate than you are at determining how much power you need to stay at a given speed. Plus, on a long car trip, you can stretch your legs a bit while driving when cruise is set.

- **Shop around for good gas prices**

  There are apps you can download that will tell you the prices of every gas station within the vicinity. With these apps, you can plan ahead. Rather than driving around on an empty fuel tank and desperate for a gas station, leave a little in the tank and look for a better price. Gas stations near freeways are notorious for higher prices, compared to others further away.

  In some places, you can get a better price by paying in cash or using debit instead of credit. If you live somewhere where those options are accepted, make sure you have enough cash for gas at the end of the week. Some gas companies also offer discounts or perks if you use their credit card to buy gas. As always, if you pay by credit, pay it off at the end of the month so they can't use compounding interest against you.

  Some grocery stores offer points off on gas when you buy a certain amount in the store. If you normally shop in one place, this might be a good deal for you.

- **Keep tires inflated & use the right oil**

  Gas mileage decreases when your tires aren't fully inflated, and it's also much safer to drive on properly inflated tires! You may be able to see if they're flat, but it's best to also check the tire pressure before you drive and when the tires are cold. The tires warm up as they roll, which will inflate the pressure reading. Inflate to the manufacturer's guidelines.

The manufacturer should have also specified the right oil to use with the car. You may find a cheaper oil; however, if it's not up to spec, it may cause damage in the long term. If you have someone change the oil, make sure they're using the right formula. Likewise, you don't necessarily have to change the oil every 3,000 miles. That was the old standard, but most cars can roll perfectly fine up to 10,000 miles or even 20,000 miles. Lease contracts may also require regular maintenance.

- No driving is the cheapest way to drive

    Needless to say, less driving also means less overall mileage and wear and tear on your car. We don't have a lot of public transportation here in the US, so most of us do have to drive. However, you can drive less by combining errands together, rather than making multiple trips. Not only are you saving money in terms of mileage, but you would also be saving time.

Medium-Term to Implement in the Next Few Months

Some of the following steps may take a little bit more planning or computing of costs, so that you can weigh advantages and disadvantages more accurately.

- If you have more than one car, decide if you really need all of them

    Two adults in a household means you need two cars, right? Well, not necessarily. Here's where you really have to spend some time thinking about it. If both of you work in opposite directions from each other, have different work schedules, and without public transportation in your area, you may need to keep both. But, what if that's not the case?

If there is a lot of public transportation near you and the places you frequent, you can probably get away with one car. This is the same as if you lived and worked near someone you could carpool with. Many families in the United States have been able to get away with having just one car, and you can too.

- Decide if it may be cheaper to keep a second car or use a taxi/ridesharing service.

  Recall that the cost of a car isn't just the upfront cost—it includes maintenance, insurance, repairs, and gas too. Even if you don't drive a single mile all year, you'll still spend hundreds on insurance, fees, and maintenance. Thus, if one of you doesn't really drive that much, do you really need that second car? Can you get by calling the occasional cab or rideshare? While someone else is driving, you can read, prep for a meeting, or just chat with the driver and enjoy the drive.

  You can also consider using a rental car service, such as Zipcar, and seeing if that can save you money. We live in an era of options and not everyone needs to own or lease a car to get around. Explore some of these other choices and see if they'd work for you, and you will also help reduce traffic associated with environmental impact.

- Perform preventative maintenance

  The best way to keep your car going for a long time is to make sure it receives preventative maintenance. Most cars have a schedule for major services: a comprehensive service at 90,000 miles, timing belt replacement (for cars that still have them), oil changes, and filter replacements.

Not getting these things done on a timely basis means a shorter life for your car. It may be money out of your pocket when you bring it to a mechanic, but it's a short-term cost that will benefit you in the long run.

- **DIY the repairs and service that you can**

    Granted, many of today's cars run on computers instead of the mechanical devices as old cars did. However, you can still look up the meanings of the various lights and icons that appear on your dashboard. Doing so can help you figure out car repairs yourself, rather than going to visit a mechanic.

    You may not have a jack to pick your car up for tire rotation maintenance; however, you should be able to at least change the oil yourself. You can also replace the windshield wipers, inflate the tires, among other repairs.

    If you're a relatively handy person, you could probably do even more—changing out the cabin or other air filters, replacing light bulbs, battery, or sundry other small parts. As with all crafts and hobbies, there are tutorials online for practically everything! Note that not all repairs should be done at home, however, and some should only be tackled by professionals.

- **Carpool when you can**

    Carpooling also allows you to do two things at once, and you will get to know people better. If you and a friend, neighbor, or colleague work in the same place or at least somewhat close to each other, carpooling works really well. You'll have some companions for the ride, which is helpful when there's a lot of traffic or a long distance. If you're not the one driving, you could probably catch up on some calls, emails, or other work-related tasks. It's also less wear and tear on everyone's vehicles because the frequency at which you drive would be less.

It may also help if you live in an area with high-occupancy vehicle (HOV) lanes, which are faster. The residents in an outer suburb of Virginia started "slugging" in one of the commuter lots. Within this transaction, people who wanted a ride would line up, and single drivers would pick up a passenger or two, thus allowing the car to drive in the HOV lane. Most office space in the area may be clustered in one spot, and it has decent public transportation for a US city. Therefore, once the car entered the main city, everyone was pretty close to their destination. This transaction would be the same coming back to the commuter lot.

Long-term planning

You might have learned some new things in the past couple of sections, but now it's time to ask the big questions. Why are you driving your specific vehicle, and should you make a switch? If you live far from where you work, should you consider making a change? Think about a different lifestyle if you're the type who leases cars.

- **Is your vehicle suited to your life? If not, trade it in.**

    Very few people have large families, haul or tow cargo regularly, or drive often into the hinterlands and off-road. Many drivers spend most of their driving time going from home to work, the mall, or a grocery store—all on paved roads.

    Pickup trucks are usually necessary in only one of two instances: when moving heavy loads or cargo, or when driving somewhere that requires a high clearance factor, such as unpaved or rocky roads. Otherwise, pickup trucks are more of a *want* rather than a *need*.

    Sport utility vehicles (SUVs) aren't really necessary unless you have a large family. They can also be quite dangerous to pedestrians and young drivers, as they can be a little more difficult to control.

The best car for most drivers are those that are small and fuel-efficient. They may not appear as cool on the surface, but they will save you a lot of money. Similar to boats, not only is a big car longer, but also wider and taller. All it requires are extra material and different construction. In other words, you will overpay larger vehicles twice—upfront when you buy it and during its life—for higher consumption and regular expenses.

Electric cars are great for gas mileage, but the infrastructure for electric cars is spotty. One city may have excellent facilities for electric vehicles, whereas another an hour away may have nothing. In that case, a hybrid may be a better option. You can choose a plug-in hybrid, though it may be better if you have a house or garage where you can plug it in overnight. Otherwise, you can choose an old-school hybrid that charges its battery through braking. Even a small, non-hybrid car will be more fuel-efficient than a large car. Having a smaller car will also limit how much you can put in it, increasing your gas mileage.

- **Buy used**

    A new car doesn't really have to be brand-new, just new to you. You can let someone else handle the cost of the depreciation.

    Make sure it's a good value, though. Pull the reports using its vehicle identification Number (VIN) to see if it's been in any accidents that might cause long-term damage. You'll want to know if it was previously a rental car or fleet vehicle, as cars with these histories were usually not taken care of well, neither by the owners nor the users. The fastest car will have been a company car.

    You can consider asking a mechanic friend to check it out. Another option is to buy a certified "preowned" vehicle from a dealership. They normally come with a warranty that can protect the car even further.

- **Consider moving to a place that's closer to work, or one that has better public transportation.**

  If you live far from work and commute every day, it isn't just about the wear and tear on your car, but that on you and your family too. In my book *Work from Home During and After the Coronavirus*, I describe trending remote job opportunities for freelancers and entrepreneurs from home. 46% of freelancers chose to work remotely because of personal circumstances, such as caring for children or other relatives, or if they have health limitations and disabilities (Upwork, 2020).[16]

  Perhaps you moved out to a suburb because the house had a yard and single bedrooms for the kids. However, you may never have time to spend with the kids because you're gone before they go to school in the morning, and you don't come back until it's dark. Is a long commute the best use of your time? What if you moved to a smaller house that was closer? In that case, you could eat breakfast with the kids and maybe have time to play with them before it gets dark. It won't kill the kids to share bedrooms.

  Don't have kids? You could still use the extra time to yourself or with your partner if you have one.

  There are other cases that this advice would alleviate, such as bad traffic during your commute or if your kids need to be supervised when playing outside in your specific environment. You could also consider living where there's good public transportation. Such communities tend to be walkable and have more of a "togetherness" feel.

- **Stop leasing cars every couple of years**

  If you lease cars, you are spending too much money without benefiting from an asset. Again, think wants and needs—no one needs a new car every two years. If you like variety, pick something that's cheaper to change out every few years, like the upholstery on your chairs or the paint on the walls.

Ending a lease early can be very expensive, so you may need to wait until the end of the term if you decide to stop leasing. At the end, you can trade in for another lease, turn it in, then walk away or buy the car you've been leasing. If you buy that car, you're probably spending too much (Swartz, 2020).[17] You might owe some fees in the end, especially if there was excessive wear and tear. Make sure you give them back everything the car came with (mats, key fobs, etc.)

Cars on the road today can go well over 100 thousand miles, thus the cost you pay to buy them amortizes itself over the years. I once bought a 2004 Mazda Miata new for about $26,000 and drove it for 13 years until the head gasket blew. At that point, it wasn't worth the repair cost, so I bought a used car to replace it.

The $26K over 13 years can calculate to $2,000 a year. In other words, the cost amortized to less than $170/month over the life of the car, which is a lot less than what a lease goes for these days! I'd taken out a 5-year loan to pay for it, and, once it was paid off, I had no car payment. Think about having a car payment of $0 for 8 years—it's pretty sweet! You can also save up the amount of that car payment and be ready to go for a new-to-you car in cash once you've driven the old one into the ground.

Chapter Summary

- Not everyone needs to own a car, and some people may have other vehicles they don't use enough to justify the costs of maintenance and repair.
- Drivers can sell vehicles they don't need immediately and reduce gas costs by making adjustments to how they drive and the cargo they carry.
- In one to three months, consider selling off a second car if you can get by without it through carpooling, rideshare, taxis, or transit, and doing as much DIY servicing and repair as you can to your current car.
- Over the long term, think about the kind of vehicle your household truly needs, and replace it when necessary with a used vehicle instead of a brand new one.

In the next chapter, we'll discuss how to reduce your clothing costs, even if you must wear business dress to work.

---

[15] https://afdc.energy.gov/files/u/publication/gas-saving_tips_july_2013.pdf

[16] https://www.upwork.com/press/2019/10/03/freelancing-in-america-2019/

[17] https://www.policygenius.com/loans/what-happens-at-the-end-of-a-car-lease/

DANA WISE

Chapter SEVEN

DRESS TO IMPRESS (YOUR WALLET)

CLOTHING is definitely necessary; however, you don't have to buy designer clothes. You also don't have to purchase "fast fashion" that is bad for both the environment and workers who make it. You might be thinking that it's impossible to dress well on a budget or without resorting to cheap clothing designed to fall apart after a few spins in the washing machine. The reality is that it actually isn't, and this book contains some tips on maintaining your current wardrobe, so you won't have to constantly replenish it.

Quick Tips to Start Now

We've got tips on what you can do right now during social distancing. These tips may even give you something interesting to do while you can't go out and shop.

- **Implement a buy-nothing plan**

    This has a very simple premise: commit to buying nothing, including shopping online. Most of us have too many clothes and only wear a fraction of our wardrobe anyway.

    You may need to replace items that wear out faster, such as underwear, but decide that you will not buy anything new for a set time. Try for at least six months, if not a year. That decision will carry you through the months until the stores open back up. Avoid the temptation.

- **Sell clothes you don't need if possible and take designer items to consignment**

    Do you have anything you never wear? Maybe it's too small, big, or it makes you feel older. If any of your clothes have stains that won't come out, toss or cut them up for rags. No one will accept stained clothes. In general, there's no point in holding on to any of these items.

    Have designer items in good condition? You can try checking out consignment shops instead. Once the garment sells, the shop owner will give you a part of the proceeds. In this transaction, you may end up with more money than if you sold outright—that way, the owner won't have to come up with the cash.

    You can also try auction sites online or resale shops if you want to sell any of your old clothes.

- **Make small repairs where necessary so you can wear clothes again**

    If you have clothes that need little repairs to be either wearable or sellable, now's the time. It will really benefit you if you spend some time working on them.

Sew on buttons, fix unraveled hems, and reinforce rips along the seams. If you're creative, you could even think of ways to repurpose the item into something different. Consider adding decorative trim or thread, changing out the buttons, and refreshing a tired wardrobe. You might end up with almost an entirely new wardrobe for close to nothing in the end!

- **Don't wash too often, and don't throw things in the dryer**

    Get in the habit of extending the life of your clothing. Washers and dryers, especially commercial ones in apartment buildings, tend to be extremely harsh on your clothes. If you didn't get your clothing dirty when you wore it, you probably don't need to wash it. A better alternative for your clothes is hanging it up and letting it air out instead of throwing it straight in the laundry. Note that white shirts may be the exception, as they tend to discolor quickly around the armpits.

    Likewise, try to avoid using the dryer when you can. Many people need to dry their sheets, towels, and other household items; however, clothing can be hung up instead. You should especially consider this if you have an outdoor area where they can dry your clothes in the fresh air. If not, find a spot inside where your clothes can rest until they're dried.

    Not only does this tactic save money in the long term by making your wardrobe last longer. It also saves money because you won't be washing and drying as much, meaning fewer dollars into the commercial machines or lower water and electric bills, depending on where you do your laundry.

Medium-Term to Implement in the Next Few Months

Once social distancing orders have ended, you can probably try some wardrobe changes. How is that possible with a buy-nothing plan and not overspending? Once again, it's time to get creative!

- Clothing swaps with friends

    These can be a lot of fun once we can gather together again. You can do this at someone's house or at your own—invite your friends over and have them bring clean clothing they're willing to trade. Consider also bringing your own drinks and make it a real party. You would still end the night with some new clothes—at least, new to you.

- Yard sales

    Sometimes, your entire neighborhood may decide to have a yard sale. If they do, go up and down the street and check out what your neighbors have to offer. These events are particularly great for kids' clothes because there are usually older kids who want to sell old clothes they've outgrown. No matter the reason, some clothes will be perfect for your kids.

    Yard sales work for finding household items and adult clothing too. You never know what you'll find! People may have been hiding clothes that don't fit them in the back of their closet, so you may even find clothes that have never been worn.

    In some cases, people set up yard sales because they're moving or found they had too much stuff in their house. Check local listings and handmade signs that can direct you toward a house with sales. You can also have your own yard sale showcasing items you no longer need. You will not only earn some money, but you will also get to learn more about your neighbors while having a bit of fun.

- Browse without bringing your wallet

    Are you one of those people who just enjoy shopping? Do you like to see what's out there or how others put outfits together? All of that is completely fine, and you might even get some great ideas for your own wardrobe!

The problem lies in your likeliness to actually shop when you browse. To avoid temptation, don't bring your wallet with you while shopping—leave it at home instead. You could also try locking it in the glove box of your car and parking far away from where you plan to window shop. Once you have your preventative measures in place, you can then browse to your heart's content, taking in various wardrobe ideas without worrying about spending money. If you see something you really like, by the time you leave, the desire will have worn off.

- **When buying, make sure the clothes don't need special care**

    Dry cleaning is expensive. The chemicals used are extremely toxic, and green cleaners may also be too expensive. When you're buying clothes you plan to wear often, avoid those with a "dry clean only" label because you will spend too much cleaning them.

    Instead, make sure it can go in the washer. Business suits tend to be dry-clean only, but you shouldn't have to clean them after every wearing. Some brands make suits that can be tossed in the laundry, so check for these options first.

- **Care for your clothes, so they can last longer**

    This is why you shouldn't buy dry-clean-only clothes: they'll wear out faster if you put them in the laundry! The more you can abide by the garment label, the longer your clothing will last, assuming you haven't been purchasing fast-fashion items that are designed to fall apart after one season. As a general rule, if you see a hole, mend it if you can.

    When you do need to do laundry, it's often helpful to turn the item inside out, as long as you don't have stains on the front. Doing so keeps your clothes looking new longer, as the washing machine agitation can be harsh.

You don't necessarily need fabric softener sheets, which are bad for the environment and can be expensive. You can use a laundry ball of foil, tennis ball, felted wool ball, or plastic hedgehog dryer ball to soften and prevent static cling.

Wash your woolen items carefully and reshape them to dry. You'll need to lay them flat in most cases. Use a laundry bag for delicates, so they don't wind around the agitator. Make sure to pretreat stains or try to dab them out immediately, so you don't have to give up on a garment just because you spilled something on it.

- **Shop out of season**

    If you do need to replace items, try to shop out of season and when they're cheapest. Stores charge high prices at the beginning of the season, so expect to pay the price if you're looking for a new swimsuit just before summer. Thus, you can try buying at the end of the season. Though the variety won't be there, some good deals may be while stores make way for new merchandise.

- **Buy on sale**

    Planning ahead helps prevent mindless spending. If you know you need a certain item, give yourself some time before you buy. Wait to see if you can find it on sale; that way, you're not forced to buy something at full price.

    Try to use coupons too, if you have any. Using a store credit card often works and it may give you a discount; however, you must pay it off at the end of the month. Do not allow your clothing purchases to be used against you in terms of incurring interest! If you don't have the cash to buy it, then you can't afford it.

Long-Term Planning

Having a vision for your wardrobe and plan to achieve that vision may sound a little silly. Nevertheless, you'll end up saving a lot of money now and in the long run when you make a plan for what you wear. Some people are creative and like expressing that through their clothing. You can still be creative and save money.

- **Wardrobe planning**

    Planning does not have to be boring. In fact, if you're the creative type, challenge yourself to find fewer pieces to mix and match when making different outfits. Matchy-matchy is no longer in fashion. If you take your clothes out of the closet and pile them up, you can probably find several yards of fabric, giving you many options to mix. If you have business suits that you no longer wear, you can break them up into individual pieces and wear them with different items.

    If you don't want to express your creativity through your clothes—and there are people who don't—you can consider a uniform. Think about Steve Jobs's iconic black turtleneck; he didn't spend a lot of time dressing in the morning because he always knew what he was going to wear. You may not want to wear a black turtleneck everyday yourself, but maybe your "uniform" is a pair of black pants and a collared shirt in colors you like to wear. Choose what you feel comfortable in.

    Having neutrals such as navy, black, and camel in your wardrobe means that you don't have to buy as many clothes. Use them as your staples, and no one will know that you're wearing your black pants twice in one week. Who can tell?

    Think *capsule collection*, which is just a term for basics that are timeless. You can mix in accessories and more seasonal pieces as you feel the need to be more creative. However, the backbone of your wardrobe will never go out of style.

- **Reassess stores: think consignments, thrifts, and renting special occasion**

  Where are you buying your clothes? You don't necessarily need to go to the mall—consignment and thrifts stores are more likely to have classic pieces by manufacturers that are not designed to fall apart after a few months. They're also great places to shop for your basics, along with some more creative options. The clothes may not be this season's fashion, but you shouldn't worry too much about that. You can gain your own creative style through it or base your wardrobe on timeless classics. Neither of these options are subject to the whims of fashion. Designer clothing can be extremely well-made. Though you may spend more at a consignment store, if you take care of your item, it can last forever.

  The trick to thrift and consignment stores is their location. People tend to donate clothes locally, so if you live on the less expensive end of town, you may not find a lot of quality clothing in your thrift store. Therefore, you will need to dig for it. If you travel toward a wealthier section of town, you'll probably find a bigger selection of high-quality clothing. You may find higher price tags, but it'll still be cheaper than buying new.

  Direct purchases from China will also often be the cheapest. They do not have seasons for two reasons—first, they sell globally, since spring in North America is autumn in Australia. Second, you pay for production and shipping costs without expensive intermediators.

  When it comes to special occasions, such as white or black tie events, consider renting your wardrobe rather than buying it. Women will often only wear dresses for these events once, and the dresses are not cheap. Likewise, men who often attend black-tie events might buy theirs because they may have more use for their suits. Decide if you should be renting or buying, and you will save a lot of money.

- **List anything that's missing from your wardrobe and plan to purchase only that item**

    Once you have your wardrobe plan, you will know if you're missing anything. For example, you might need a coat or blazer if you don't already have one. Since you're planning ahead, you're giving yourself time. Thus, it is time to check the thrift shops and see if they have what you need. Look at coupons and sales for higher quality items and pounce if you find a good price.

    Having a list prevents you from buying things you don't need and mindlessly spending. When you go to the store, you're laser-focused on one specific item; if the item you need isn't there, make a quick exit and go on to the next store.

- **If something comes in, something has to go out**

    Not only will this rule help you declutter your closet, but it will also help you be mindful about your spending. You might end up shopping and browsing through the store and find something that you don't really need or that doesn't fit with your plan. Before purchase, ask yourself what you would get rid of if you bought this item. Doing so gives you the space you need to be mindful about the potential purchase. Do you really need this item? If you don't think you can replace anything with it, you might not need it.

    In another scenario, maybe earlier you bought something intentionally that just didn't quite work out. Perhaps the fabric was too scratchy, or you kept tugging at the lapel. The one-in-one-out rule will help you get rid of it instead of letting it clutter your closet, thus you can replace it with an item that fits your lifestyle better.

Chapter Summary

- You don't have to spend too much money to have a great wardrobe.
- Implement a buy-nothing plan right away and use your time during this pandemic to make any needed repairs.
- In the next few months, have swaps with friends or pick up items you need at a yard sale.
- Plan ahead for your wardrobe and shop only to fill in the gaps in the future.
- Create your own style.

In the next chapter, we will go over some tips for traveling on a budget that will still allow you to enjoy that trip!

DANA WISE

Chapter EIGHT

TRAVEL TIGHT

RIGHT now, you might not even be thinking about traveling! By contrast, you could be dreaming about taking a vacation once the pandemic is over. The good news is that you can still have an enjoyable trip even while watching your money. There's a lot of information about how to plan and execute a frugal yet wonderful vacation, and now is a great time to start dreaming and planning for a terrific trip.

Quick Tips to Start Now

What kind of trip are you planning to take? There are tons of things you can do, including sightseeing, doing physical activities, and relaxing on the beach. What sounds good to you?

- **Consider switching to travel rewards credit cards**

    The vast majority of credit and debit cards offer some kind of reward. Do you know what kind of rewards yours have? Do some research on your credit or debit card's company to see the kinds of bonus offers your cards give you. If your cards don't include travel rewards, consider switching to ones that do. Go online to find a card that offers good travel rewards and has a low or nonexistent annual fee—preferably zero!

    A no-fee credit card won't give you concierge perks, but that's not what you're looking for. You're looking for one that offers good travel rewards, so don't let yourself get sidetracked with "deals" that aren't meaningful to you.

- **Plan ahead of time & savor the anticipation**

    Do you know why now is the perfect time to start planning? It turns out that the biggest pleasure in traveling is actually the anticipation (Andrews, 2018).[18] Studies have found that we're happiest leading up to an event. On some occasions, we are happier than we are during the event, and usually when looking back on it.

    With all this free time now, you can start dreaming and thinking about your next event. Savor that anticipation and use this early start to start planning. You'll have a better idea of what you're looking for and can keep an eye out for money-saving opportunities that may arise.

Medium-Term to Implement in the Next Few Months

This is the time to dive into research and planning, now you have a good idea of what you would like to do and what would be best for you.

- **Research**

    Planning is part of the fun and anticipation, and you can save a lot of money doing it! Once you've figured out where you want to go, look into attractions you can visit. If you can, find some free and low-cost activities. Remember from a previous chapter that some museums have free days, so you can add those attractions to your itinerary. There may also be some free festivals or holiday extravaganzas. What looks interesting, fun, and different? Are there any free or low-cost ways for you to take advantage of them? Make sure you include those considerations in your trip.

    A great way to save money is to go during the off-season. Everyone goes to New York during Christmas, which is both expensive and crowded. Therefore, find a different season to go. Likewise, make sure that the attractions you want to visit will be open during the time you go. For example, August in Paris is off-season, but everyone's on vacation for the month, meaning nothing will be open.

    Although exchange rates vary throughout the year and you don't have a lot of control over them, try to take them into account when planning. If the rate is bad for a certain country, you may want to postpone your trip until it becomes a bit more favorable.

- **Use coupons, deals, loyalty programs, and credit card rewards**

    If you travel a lot for business and have gained many points with airlines or chains, use those for your vacation. If you can find deals and coupons for your intended destination, use those too. Hopefully, you can also implement some credit card rewards now too!

    I have used these tricks myself; I traveled to Macchu Picchu in Peru using credit card rewards and airline miles once. I used a low-cost outfitter and shared a tent on the trail. The group I went with all became good friends after one week together, and we learned so much by having a native guide for the trip. I could have spent a lot more money and stayed in more luxurious surroundings, but my more frugal methods led to one of the most memorable trips I'd ever taken. Similarly, I took a service trip with the Sierra Club. My group did some physical work in the park, and I learned a lot and paid *much* less than if I'd gone with a tour group.

So, get creative! That's how you get memorable trips.

- **Be open to change if it's cheaper**

   Flexibility is the key to cheap travel; for example, the airline cost might be significantly less if you leave or return on a different day, or use a different airport. You could also opt to make some slight changes to your itinerary if some other money-saving opportunity arises. Keep an eye out for last-minute deals to your destination.

   However, you'll want to stick with one airline and its business partners; otherwise, you might miss your connection if you come in late and communication between the flights is spotty.

- **Avoid package deals if you don't plan to take advantage of part of the package**

   Cruise lines may offer very luxurious packages, along with some all-inclusive resorts. However, if you don't take advantage of everything they offer, the ideal may not turn out to be so wonderful after all.

   For example, suppose you don't drink alcohol. Does it make sense to go to an all-inclusive resort where one of the biggest benefits is all-you-can-drink alcohol? That is the same on a cruise line. If you're not a very active person, does it make sense to travel on a huge ship where the biggest attraction is the variety of physical activities contained in the offer? Probably not.

- **Explore locally**

    Have you explored your area much? Rather than flying or cruising—both of which are pretty bad for the environment—consider driving somewhere near you. Most states have some nice parks that you may have yet to visit or have only visited a part of.

    What nearby attractions have you seen but never been to? Are there any interesting festivals that you could check out within a day's drive or so? Members of AAA receive a monthly magazine that lists interesting events happening nearby, and you can also check out events online.

    Maybe you can't afford a big trip every year. Nevertheless, that doesn't mean you can't have a little vacation more often. Use your vacation days and take an interesting and fun break more often and when you can't take a big one.

- **Consider more interesting accommodations**

    Hotels can be expensive—fortunately, there exist many other less expensive options! Bed and breakfasts, short-term rentals, hostels, and even swapping your home with someone else can all be cheaper and more fun options than a boring corporate hotel.

    Make sure you open up your search to include non-hotel options. As a bonus, you will have the opportunity to see non-touristy places and how the locals live, or try some unique food.

Long-Term Planning

Great—now that you've done all your research, what's next?

- **Save up**

    Do you have enough cash saved to finance your trip? If not, you can't afford that trip. This doesn't mean, however, that you have to pay for everything in cash! It just means that you may want to wait a little longer before you take that vacation.

The savings you've been making along the way in your budget should help. You just don't want to put your trip on your credit card, then be unable to pay it off when you get back.

o **Be smart when you reach your destination**

Rather than eating out at restaurants all the time, go grocery shopping for food. The bonus will be that you get to meet local people and not just other tourists eating in the restaurants. You may also get to eat what the locals do.

You'll probably want to bring home some souvenirs that will remind you of your lovely trip, but don't overspend. Buy something that's meaningful from the place you're visiting and that fits your budget—not the cheapest junk in the shop or something you can get at home.

I had a friend who loved jewelry, and she would always buy a pair of earrings from the street vendors when she traveled. When she got home, no one else was wearing the same thing.

o **Budget for a splurge or two, but not the whole time**

When you're in Paris, you will obviously go to eat at a romantic restaurant. Likewise, you will probably go to a Broadway show when you're in New York (with half-price tickets if you buy the day of the show) or visit the beer garden in certain areas of Germany.

Don't splurge every day, but when you do decide to splurge, enjoy it! It's a treat.

o **Find a vacation that combines two concepts**

You want to relax on the beach, but you also want to do some fun activities; therefore, find a spot where you can do both. You may need to drive a bit to reach your second destination, but it'll be worth it.

Chapter Summary

- Travel and fun do not have to be expensive.
- Start dreaming and planning now because anticipation is the best part of the trip!
- In the next few months, do your research and plan a wonderful and inexpensive trip, which doesn't have to be overseas.
- On your trip, you can plan for a splurge or two, but be smart at your destination.

In the next chapter, we will discuss how to create a wonderful and inexpensive future today.

---

[18] https://www.nathab.com/blog/anticipation-is-the-happiest-part-of-a-travel-journey/

Chapter NINE

CREATE YOUR FUTURE TODAY

NOW it's time to put everything together! There are a lot of ways to save money that we've listed in this book, and it's OK if you're feeling a little overwhelmed! Maybe you've seen some of the information before, though much of it is still new. If you haven't started your journey yet, here's how you can finally put your plan into action.

Remember to take deep breaths and let your reasoning brain take over! Money and finances often make people stress out, so make sure you're calm and not feeling too anxious. Taking action makes your brain happy, and planning is the first step to take. Here's how you can really make a difference in saving your money.

The following ten steps will change your life, so read through them first to see how the system works. Then, come on back and start taking action on step one. Once you decide to put these into place, you'll start saving money. Reading is great, but the only way you can make big changes is by taking action!

1. **Determine where you are now**

   Choose a free expense-tracking app and get started. They're all pretty much the same, so don't spend a lot of time picking one. The apps can't necessarily go back in time and pick up earlier spending, so this is where some homework comes in.

   Gather up your credit and debit card statements, your checking statement, and receipts—a spreadsheet is probably the easiest way to enter all these expenses. Hopefully, you can export everything from your credit card companies, so then you can copy and paste those into the spreadsheet. Categorize the spending if it's not already done for you: groceries, entertainment, car, etc. You can then choose categories from chapters 2-8 or your own, whichever you prefer.

   Having three months is best. That way, you can average them out, as one month might be especially high or low for a specific reason. Averaging the three months gives you a pretty good estimate of what you're actually spending. Once you've done all that, total the amount you've spent in each category, along with the total for the month.

2. **Pick a category to start**

   This book is organized into the following categories: food, home, wired services, entertainment, vehicles, wardrobe, and travel.

   Start with an easy topic, where you know you can make a difference right away by dropping a product or service, or selling something. In some subjects, you may already know where you tend to overspend.

3. **Go back to that chapter and read the suggestions**

    Which of the chapters is applicable to you? For example, in the chapter about your home, there are suggestions for both renters and homeowners. If you own your house, the renter suggestions won't apply to you, and vice versa.

    Which ones can you commit to taking right now or within the next one to three months? Are there any long-term ideas that you can commit to or consider right now? Think about these questions.

4. **Write down the steps you want to take**

    You will need to get out a paper and pen for this one. I still write things down, as writing things down helps to clarify and prioritize things for yourself. It will make you feel less anxious because your brain isn't tasked with trying to maintain that note too. Writing rather than typing has been shown to help us both remember and process things better (Doubek, 2016).[19] Therefore, whichever steps you've decided to take, write them down. Another benefit of writing them down is that, when you complete the step, you can cross it off, which is very satisfying.

    I created a one page form that will come in handy for tracking every saving, from planning to recording the results, and with instructions for filling out each section. If you have yet to download it, please use the link that you find in the beginning of this book right after the Table of Contents.

    Give yourself a deadline for each step. For example, if you want to call your service providers, give yourself three days to do it. Then, put it in your calendar or task list, so you can have a reminder that it's due.

    Who else needs to be involved in the step? Do you need some sort of agreement or help from your spouse, like with selling the car? Estimate the savings for these steps.

5. Write SMART goals for longer-term plans

The suggestions for the long term tend to require more planning, or at least more consideration on your part. You can think in terms of SMART goals: Specific, Measurable, Achievable, Relevant and Time-bound.

Maybe you're considering moving. What actions do you need to achieve this goal? You'll need to research your potential location and all associated costs, and calculate your commute fees and wear and tear. When will you have the research done? When will you be able to make the decision? Write down the small steps that will help you reach your goal, then put those into your calendar too.

6. Write down the positive effects of taking these actions

You don't want to feel deprived! In addition, if you keep thinking negatively in terms of what you're cutting back, you will probably feel that way. It may not be a great idea now out of excitement for potential savings, but down the line, consider what it is you're achieving so you can avoid binging and splurging.

Taking action isn't just positive for your wallet, but you'll also get to exercise some creativity, even if you hadn't done so in a while! You may uncover new skills or abilities during this ordeal. How beautiful is it to enjoy the present moment without worrying about whether your car, house, or spouse is as nice as your neighbors or friends? You won't be worrying about having to maintain a standard of living and spending more time with friends and family. You will get to spend your precious time with your loved ones instead of watching TV.

Write down the positive effects, along with the next-order consequences. Now that you're saving more, you can pay off debts, build up an emergency fund, or plan something on your bucket list. Whatever it is, write it down. Really explore the positive changes these savings will make on your life.

7. **Take at least one short-term action**

    You know your brain loves action. Planning is key, but implementing is even more crucial, so start small and pick a quick win. Most of these short-term suggestions don't require too much work or thought.

    Once you've taken the action, you may have gained an immediate savings number. For example, if you negotiated a discount on services, you'll be paying some amount less than you were before, which you will want to write down. On the other hand, there is a chance you might have previously thought that you couldn't handle your money. With that thought, you're already taking control. It doesn't have to be hard—although some of these steps may take a little more time, you've just shown yourself that you can do it! Consider sharing your experience with your friends. Not only will doing so reaffirm what you've achieved, but you may also inspire and help them.

8. **If you're having trouble, distinguish desire from necessity**

    People get stuck sometimes, and they're not quite sure what they can do to adjust their lives financially. You might even feel that some of our steps are a bit extreme, even if they aren't. The extreme is, rather, how mindlessly we may spend. Once you prioritize your goal of saving money, you will see how all the ideas make sense.

    However, when you do get stuck, go back to the fundamental difference between *want* and *need*. You need nutritious food that provides natural vitamins and minerals, and preferably either protein, fat, or fiber. Does your proposed purchase match this? If it doesn't, don't buy it because it's a want and not a need.

Sometimes, you may have to compromise when you have two conflicting needs, or you prioritize one over the other temporarily. However, most of the time, something you believe is a need really is more of a want. When you delve deep into it, you will realize that.

9. Start on another section and repeat

These techniques can be used for every category in the book! Start small and easy with quick wins you can capture right away. Doing so makes it easier in the long haul, and you will be able to say to yourself that you can do this, as you'll have proof that you can save money. Then, it's just a matter of figuring out how to do it.

10. Reflect on how much you saved

You should have some actual earnings from the quick tips you implemented, including calling service providers and selling anything you no longer need. Add up your savings and feel proud of how much you've done.

You still have plenty more to go with long-term decisions that will give you more for your money. Don't forget the smaller ones add up too.

Do you feel deprived? Or do you feel more connected, more creative, and on a more solid foundation? I bet that you're feeling pretty good right about now!

Chapter Summary

- There are a lot of ways to save money, and, although it may feel overwhelming, you can create a plan that can put all these savings in place for you.
- Start tracking your spending and determine where you are right now.
- Take one category and write down the actions you plan to take, including long-term goals.
- Pick an easy way to save money and do it!
- Continue with the other categories, implementing and calculating your savings as you go.

In the next chapter, we will go over how to stay motivated and continue saving in the future

---

[19] https://www.npr.org/2016/04/17/474525392/attention-students-put-your-laptops-away

Chapter TEN

CONTINUE SAVING

If you implemented just a few of the suggestions from this book so far, you've already saved money and are hopefully on the path to high-quality entertainment and time with family and friends. Now comes the challenging part: maintaining your new habits. Having to stay home during the crisis may have made it easier to avoid shopping and spending. However, you have made some big, positive changes that you should continue for a happier life with less spending.

Evaluate

First, take a look at what you've done so far. How much money have you saved tangibly, like in phone savings or avoiding new purchases? How much of that can you attribute to staying home due to the coronavirus? For example, suppose you normally like to window shop, and you end up buying things you don't really need. Having the stores closed means you've probably saved a lot of money because you couldn't do that. On the other hand, the lower prices you negotiated for services and the things you sold are not necessarily due to the epidemic.

Will you have difficulty not shopping once you can head to the mall again? The answer to this question is why you wrote down all the positive benefits to your new habits. It's not just about the money, but the time you have not worrying about that money. Along with that, it's also about the time you're spending with friends at the park or at their houses.

When you feel the itch to go shopping, turn back and read all those positive changes you wrote about that happened as a result of not shopping and saving your money instead. Do you want to jeopardize that? If you absolutely must go browsing, use the leave-your-wallet-behind trick we discussed, so you don't actually end up spending money.

You know by now that, when you do something pleasurable, your brain releases the feel-good neurotransmitter dopamine. In other words, your brain is saying, yes, let's do that again! Often, people get that little hit when they buy something. This dopamine hit is temporary and wears off fast. The pleasure in that purchase will probably dissipate before you even get your items to the car or see the purchase on your credit card statement.

Humans are adaptable creatures, and we adjust to new lifestyles pretty quickly. Things that originally brought us a lot of pleasure will eventually subside; for example, once most people get a raise, they will increase their spending to adjust to the new income instead of saving it. That new, shiny car is exciting when you can first afford it, but it will feel like nothing special after a while. You may have heard this referred to as the hedonic treadmill (in which "hedonic" refers to "pleasure") (Pennock, 2019).[20]

Once you get on this treadmill, it's hard to get off! That's when you're most susceptible to ads that suggest you'll be healthier, happier, or richer if you buy their product or service. One of the best ways to avoid or get off of this treadmill is to find meaning and purpose in your life. That's right—all the work you've been doing to develop new skills and spend more time with people will also help you avoid the need to buy for pleasure. Exercise, which you've probably started doing, is also a source of pleasure.

You can add that to your list of positive benefits too—that your new life, free of spending, is making you happier than your old one in which you spent too much money out of habit. If you feel like a rebel, this is an excellent way to rebel: spending more time and money on your loved ones, and less on big corporations!

Maintain Motivation

The silver lining to the crisis is that it made most of us do things differently. If you had bad habits, like hitting the coffee shop or cardboard masquerading as a sweet treat, you've been forced to break that habit. If you wandered aimlessly around the mall every Saturday morning, you've broken that habit.

Leave those habits broken—there is no need to race out once the restrictions are lifted and spend money just because you can. By now, you should have developed the habit of thinking mindfully about your expenses. Do you need or want it? If it's a want, then you probably don't need to spend money on it.

Having goals becomes more important when we can get back out there and hit the mall or the electronics store. You're not saving money just because someone told you to or financial planners say it's a good idea. If your only reason for saving money is because someone else thinks you should, there's no way you can stop spending too much over the long term.

You might be riding high on the idea of savings in the immediate future; at some point, however, you will see something you want.

Not something you need, but something that you want. When that happens, if the only thing standing between you and that purchase is how someone else told you that not spending is a good idea, you will spend like it's your last day on Earth.

However, now you're armed with your goals. You know you don't have infinite time or billions of dollars to spend and need to prioritize. It may be tempting, but you need your home and to save for that down payment. You could be paying off your credit cards or building up your emergency fund. In this case, you also would no longer be living paycheck to paycheck.

Plus, look at all the great things you did when you saved money. Your loved ones can be lots of fun! You discovered that you're really good at playing guitar, even though you haven't done it since seventh grade. You and your friends hang out after the weekly match to have fun. You're no longer a spender—you've evolved, even over this relatively short time. Your priorities have focused more on what's good for you rather than on material items. Now, you're the person who has control over their money, rather than letting their money take control of them, which is pretty cool. You're smart about your money, and you think about where you want to use them.

None of this means that you'll never spend again! Of course, you have the needs that you must satisfy, along with people to hang out with and new things to do. Some of these needs will require careful and mindful spending. If you've rediscovered playing the guitar, you might need to invest a bit in your guitar and maybe some lessons. Whatever your new hobby or craft is, you'll probably need to acquire some tools and/or materials to continue with it. This is all how you should think about your expenses going forward. What serves you and your goals? If a purchase doesn't satisfy one of these two items, you shouldn't buy it.

Future

There are some goals that you need to have for your savings and to make sure that you don't end up in a lot of credit card debt.

- **Pay off credit card debt**

    Interest compounding against you can make it hard to get out of your hole of debt once you're in it. The first thing to do, of course, is to not add any more debt to your cards. Save up for big purchases, so even if you do put them on the card to attain rewards points, you can pay them off immediately and not accrue interest.

    Most of the time, minimum payments don't cut it, and you will need to add a little extra to one card until you've paid it off. Then, add that amount to the monthly payments on the nest card until it's paid off. You'll also pay that card off faster if you tackle your high-interest card first. However, if you're easily discouraged, pick one with a small balance that you can pay off faster, then get the quick win that will motivate you to continue.

- **Emergency fund**

    You need three to six months' worth of expenses in cash to take care of any emergency that might arise. It's a little late for the coronavirus, but you can insulate yourself from a job layoff or other problem in the future by having this cash stashed away. A little is better than none, so put a small amount away and save more when you can.

- **Retirement**

    Very few workers have access to pensions anymore, so most of us will be retiring on whatever's left of Social Security and what we have saved. Therefore, you need to save! The earlier you start, the better.

Recall the Rule of 72—your portfolio doubles every 12 years if you earn 6% on average, which is a reasonable portfolio return. If you only have twelve years to save, you will only have one double. So, you would either have to save a massive amount each year over the next 12 years, or have far less money available. If you start saving in your forties and have 24 years to retirement, you will have two doubles. Likewise, if you start in your twenties, you will have at least three doubles.

Suggest that you start with $10,000, ignoring additions that will also increase the amount. Starting in your fifties: one double, $20,000. Starting in your forties: two doubles, $40,000. But in your twenties? Starting with $10,000, you will end up with $80,000 by doing nothing except investing the money and leaving it alone.

Chapter Summary

- Evaluate how much you've saved so far.
- Be mindful of your goals and what you value to keep your new saving and spending habits, even when the restrictions are over.
- Other goals for saving should include a payment of all credit card debt, creation of an emergency fund, and retirement.
- Remember that today, you are creating your future!

[20] https://positivepsychology.com/hedonic-treadmill/

DANA WISE

FINAL WORDS

WE'VE pooled various suggestions and ways to plan your savings in this book. Thus, it's important for you to continue your good money habits, even after the crisis is over. When people are back to work earning a salary and shops are open, it will be more tempting to spend money.

However, now you are in control of your money. If you started the book without a good foundation for handling your finances, now you have a strong one and know that that's key to managing your spending. It shouldn't be because someone told you to, but because, after implementing these ideas and seeing your savings grow, you know that it puts you on the path to achieving your goals. You also now recognize that money is a tool and nothing more. It's not how much you're worth as a person, and it doesn't signify how valuable you are.

After reading the book, you've gained a better grasp of how the human brain works, especially when it comes to your personal finances. When your brain feels threatened, it sets your fight-or-flight response into action, which is great for running away from the lion that's about to eat you. It is not, however, so great at making financial decisions. You've also gained some techniques for bringing your rational brain back online, so you can make better decisions by reasoning through them. You can now balance the short-term pleasure of spending with the long-term need to save and reach your goals.

A key factor in keeping your spending reasonable is to distinguish between what you want and what you need. It's necessary to spend money on necessities like shelter, food, and clothing, but you don't have to overspend, and there are numerous ways to bring various costs down.

None of us have infinite amounts of money or time, so we have to prioritize. And this is good; otherwise, we would be spending our entire lives buying things. We each have to consider our values and spend according to that. Yet, there is still no need to spend mindlessly on what's of value! For example, many of us enjoy being with our friends. However, you can hang out with your friends at other places besides the bar or expensive pro sports games. You can simply go to the park or someone's house, with a potluck and BYOB. If you and your friends love sports, most communities have amateur sports that you can watch, which are often cheaper and nostalgic. Even better would be playing a sport in a rec league or some kind of community team.

Most people also have financial goals they want to achieve, like buying a house or having a good retirement. It's good to have these in mind and written down in front of you. When you're tempted, these goals will help you remember why you're saving in the first place, making it easier to avoid falling for a gimmick.

Thinking about each purchase and coming up with creative alternatives instead of defaulting to buying things aren't just excellent ways to save lots of money, but they are also good for your mental and physical health. Being with friends and family instead of screens and expensive gadgets satisfies the basic need for human connection. Playing with your kids, pets, or friends also provides exercise that you can enjoy. In addition, it can help to be mindful about your expenses, when watching your mindfulness in other areas.

These are some of the intangible benefits of implementing the ideas from this book, but there are tangible ones too! Even small monthly savings add up significantly over time. We covered the main areas of spending for most people: food, home, cell/Internet services, entertainment, cars, clothing, and travel, and you found strategies that you can use right now, during the coronavirus pandemic. Some strategies include calling your service providers to reduce rates, shopping in your own pantry, and using cookbooks or the internet to find recipes for whatever's been hiding at the back of your cupboard.

We also provided suggestions that may take a little bit more planning or waiting on for when the country is no longer social distancing. These are the medium-term solutions, such as ordering appetizers, splitting entrees when going out to eat, or checking out yard sales if you need an item for your wardrobe.

Long-term tips in each chapter typically require even more planning. For example, you might rethink where you're living if you have a large house and long commute to work. Big houses also have big maintenance and utility bills, and long commutes don't just add wear and tear to the car, but also affect your and your family's mental health. Figuring out alternatives for that will take some research and hard conversations about what's livable and what's reasonable.

You've also learned to keep track of your expenses with free apps available online. Although old school methods included keeping receipts and spreadsheets, you should now be able to see exactly where your money goes. More importantly, you can see how much you're saving as a result of the tips you've learned from this book!

Saving and mindful spending are great techniques you can deploy over your entire life. As circumstances change, you can then have the flexibility to adapt. You might learn some new tips or find new ways to be creative with that which is important to you. Continuing to learn new things is also crucial for your mental health and growth.

The benefits of controlling your money aren't just financial—they extend to all the areas of your life. Thus, happy saving!

SAVE MONEY AND SPEND WISELY DURING AND AFTER CORONAVIRUS

Leave a Review

I would be incredibly *thankful* if you could take just 60 seconds to write a brief review on Amazon, even if it's just a few sentences.

If you have downloaded the one page form for tracking your savings, you can take a photo of one or two that you are proud of and attach it to the review. Your success will inspire and encourage many readers who may be struggling in the beginning. Please make sure you do not disclose any personal or sensitive information.

Please log into your Amazon account, then find this book *Save Money and Spend Wisely During and After Coronavirus*.

Alternatively type this link into your browser or scan the QR code: amazon.com/review/create-review?&asin=B08CTFCR67

Customer Reviews

 51

4.8 out of 5 stars ▼

5 star		94%
4 star		2%
3 star		0%
2 star		2%
1 star		2%

Share your thoughts with other customers

[Write a customer review]

See all 51 customer reviews ▸

My Other Book You Will Love

Resources

A. (2020, January 17). Are Social Media and Depression Linked | Florida Behavioral Health Center. Retrieved March 25, 2020, from https://www.bhpalmbeach.com/are-depression-and-social-media-usage-linked/

Andrews, C. G. (2019, December 31). Anticipation Is the Happiest Part of a Travel Journey. Retrieved March 28, 2020, from https://www.nathab.com/blog/anticipation-is-the-happiest-part-of-a-travel-journey/

A.P.T. |. (2017, February 20). 8 Powerful Benefits of Writing Things Down. Retrieved March 28, 2020, from https://www.productiveandfree.com/blog/writing-things-down-benefits

Bradford, A. (2017, March 7). Dishwasher vs. hand-washing: What saves more water? Retrieved March 25, 2020, from https://www.cnet.com/how-to/how-much-water-do-dishwashers-use/

Carinsurance.com. (2012, July 27). Don't Insure an Old Car Like a New One. Retrieved March 25, 2020, from https://www.nasdaq.com/articles/dont-insure-an-old-car-like-a-new-one-2012-07-27

Carney PHC. (2019, February 14). Using Those Ceiling Fans to Help Heat Your Home. Retrieved March 25, 2020, from https://www.carneyphc.com/blog/heating/using-ceiling-fans-help-heat-home/

Crank, J. (2019, November 12). How Much Can You Save By Adjusting Your Thermostat? Retrieved March 25, 2020, from https://www.directenergy.com/blog/how-much-can-you-save-by-adjusting-your-thermostat/

Department of Health & Human Services. (2016, August 10). The dangers of sitting: why sitting is the new smoking. Retrieved March 25, 2020, from https://www.betterhealth.vic.gov.au/health/healthyliving/the-dangers-of-sitting

Doubek, J. (2016, April 17). Attention Students: Put Your Laptops Away. Retrieved March 28, 2020, from https://choice.npr.org/index.html?origin=https://www.npr.org/2016/04/17/474525392/attention-students-put-your-laptops-away

Duke, A. (2018). Thinking in Bets. Zaltbommel, Netherlands: Van Haren Publishing.

Elkins, K. (2019, October 18). Economists say this is the minimum amount of money you need in an emergency fund. Retrieved March 25, 2020, from https://www.cnbc.com/2019/10/18/minimum-amount-of-money-you-need-in-an-emergency-fund.html

Finke, M. (2016, January 21). Old Age and the Decline in Financial Literacy. Retrieved March 25, 2020, from https://pubsonline.informs.org/doi/10.1287/mnsc.2015.2293

Goleman, D. (2009). Emotional Intelligence. Zaltbommel, Netherlands: Van Haren Publishing.

Gu, K. (2019, July 3). Can People Send and Receive Text Messages via VoIP? Retrieved March 25, 2020, from https://www.genvoice.net/can-people-send-and-receive-text-messages-via-voip/

Hunt, M. (2016, July 14). Wash Clothes Inside Out and Other Laundry Tips and Tricks. Retrieved March 28, 2020, from https://www.creators.com/read/everyday-cheapskate/07/16/wash-clothes-inside-out-and-other-laundry-tips-and-tricks

IRS. (n.d.). Standard Mileage Rates | Internal Revenue Service. Retrieved March 25, 2020, from https://www.irs.gov/tax-professionals/standard-mileage-rates

Kahneman, D. (2011). Thinking, Fast and Slow. Amsterdam, Netherlands: Adfo Books.

LaPonsie, M. (2019, August 5). Best 5 Expense Tracker Apps. Retrieved March 25, 2020, from https://money.usnews.com/money/personal-finance/saving-and-budgeting/articles/best-expense-tracker-apps

Mcleod, S. (2020, March 20). Maslow's Hierarchy of Needs. Retrieved March 25, 2020, from https://www.simplypsychology.org/maslow.html

Nottingham, P. *(2017, March 15)*. **Your Business's Videos Should Include Faces. Here's Why.** *Retrieved March 25, 2020, from https://wistia.com/learn/marketing/power-of-faces-in-video*

Pennock, S. *(2019, February 11)*. **The Hedonic Treadmill - Are We Forever Chasing Rainbows?** *Retrieved March 28, 2020, from https://positivepsychology.com/hedonic-treadmill/*

Price, C. *(2019, February 21)*. **Trapped - the secret ways social media is built to be addictive (and what you can do to fight back).** *Retrieved March 25, 2020, from https://www.sciencefocus.com/future-technology/trapped-the-secret-ways-social-media-is-built-to-be-addictive-and-what-you-can-do-to-fight-back/*

Sitlers. *(2019, November 4)*. **Choose the Right LED Color Temperature for You!** . *Retrieved March 25, 2020, from https://sitlersledsupplies.com/choose-right-led-color-temperature/*

Stahl, A. *(2018, August 12)*. **Here's How Creativity Actually Improves Your Health.** *Retrieved March 25, 2020, from https://www.forbes.com/sites/ashleystahl/2018/07/25/heres-how-creativity-actually-improves-your-health/#18d6ba0913a6*

Swartz, A. *(2020, January 7)*. **What happens at the end of a car lease.** *Retrieved March 25, 2020, from https://www.policygenius.com/loans/what-happens-at-the-end-of-a-car-lease/*

Upwork. *(2019, November 15)*. **Sixth annual "Freelancing in America" study finds that more people than ever see freelancing as a long-term career path.** *Retrieved March 28, 2020, from https://www.upwork.com/press/2019/10/03/freelancing-in-america-2019/*

US Dep't of Energy. *(n.d.)*. **Gas Saving Tips.** *Retrieved March 25, 2020, from https://afdc.energy.gov/files/u/publication/gas-saving_tips_july_2013.pdf*

US Dep't of Energy. *(n.d.)*. **Lighting Controls.** *Retrieved March 25, 2020, from https://www.energy.gov/energysaver/save-electricity-and-fuel/lighting-choices-save-you-money/lighting-controls*

Viscera. *(2017, March 16)*. **Minimalism Series: What's a Capsule Collection?** *Retrieved March 28, 2020, from https://shopviscera.com/blogs/happenings/minimalism-series-whats-a-capsule-collection*

SAVE MONEY AND SPEND WISELY DURING AND AFTER CORONAVIRUS

Dana Wise

SAVE MONEY AND SPEND WISELY DURING AND AFTER CORONAVIRUS

2020

www.ingramcontent.com/pod-product-compliance
Lightning Source LLC
Chambersburg PA
CBHW020537080526
44583CB00013B/891